WHAT READERS ARE SAYING

"In this deeply personal memoir, Lex shares a remarkable testimony of God's unfailing mercy and steadfast goodness throughout the many trials and tests of life. Woven with honesty, humility, and hope, his story demonstrates that when we fully surrender our lives to the Lord, His strength is revealed and His glory shines most brightly through our weakness. This book is a powerful reminder that no matter how dark the journey may seem, God is ever faithful, His promises endure, and He will never fail those who place their trust in Him."

Daphne Yang
Deputy Senior Pastor,
Cornerstone Community Church, Singapore
Director, The Bible College of Wales, UK

"Lex has done well in putting together his journey with God and how God's mercy has been shown in his life. From where he started to where he is now, he is a living testimony of God's blessings. I trust that his story will encourage and inspire many readers to see God's faithfulness in their own lives."

Joseph Goh, MBA
Managing Director, DLM Pte Ltd

"Some books inform. Others inspire. This book does both, for it points us to the faithfulness of God in every season of life. Through Lex's journey, we catch a glimpse of a God who never leaves, never forsakes, and never ceases to work in the lives of His children.

May these pages speak a word in season, strengthen your faith, stir your hope, and lead you to encounter for yourself the same God who is still speaking, still leading, and writing extraordinary stories through ordinary lives."

Kevin Koh

Executive Pastor, Cornerstone Community Church, Singapore

"*What You Say, Daddy?* is a deeply moving testimony of faith, surrender, and the nearness of God in life's darkest seasons. With honesty and courage, Lex Khoo invites readers into his journey of brokenness, loss, miracles, and restoration; reminding us that even when life feels uncertain, our Heavenly Father is still present, still speaking, and still revealing His glory in the dark.

What moved me most is the childlike posture carried throughout this book, the simple yet profound cry: "What You say, Daddy?" In a world crowded with fear, noise, striving, and many competing voices, Lex points us back to the one Voice that truly anchors the soul. This book will strengthen anyone carrying silent questions, praying through tears, or needing fresh hope to keep going."

Sharon Chong

Founder, Head Coach, Speaker GenBrave International

"*What You Say, Daddy?* is more than a collection of testimonies; it is a beautiful invitation to trust the voice of God in every season of life. Honest, faith-filled, and deeply encouraging, Lex's story reminds us that our greatest hope is found in Jesus, who remains faithful through every valley and every victory."

Andrew Yeo
Pastor, Cornerstone Community Church, Singapore

"Having known Lex for more than twenty years as a dear friend, brother in Christ, and faithful leader, I have witnessed the authenticity of the life behind these pages.

What You Say, Daddy? is not simply a collection of testimonies; it is the courageous and deeply moving account of a man who encountered Jesus in his darkest moments and learned to live by the voice of his Heavenly Father.

With humility, honesty, and childlike faith, Lex reminds us that Jesus is near in our brokenness, faithful through every valley, and still able to restore what seems beyond repair. This book will strengthen the weary, awaken hope in those carrying silent pain, and invite every reader to lean in afresh and ask, "Daddy, what are You saying?"

I warmly commend it to all who desire to encounter the Father's love and the transforming power of a life surrendered to Christ."

Timothy Chong
Pastor, Cornerstone Community Church, Singapore

"*What You Say, Daddy?* is a deeply heartfelt and faith-filled testimony of God's presence through brokenness, surrender, healing, and restoration. With honesty and humility, Lex Khoo shares his journey in a way that points readers back to the faithfulness of Jesus and the loving voice of the Heavenly Father in every season of life. This book will encourage anyone who needs fresh hope, renewed faith, and the reminder that God is still near, still speaking, and still at work in the darkest moments."

Jeff Yuen
Pastor, Cornerstone Community Church, Singapore

"I have known Lex since he first joined our cell in church. From the very beginning, he has been a man of unwavering faith, following God with wholehearted surrender. His obedience has led him to distant lands and bold ventures, each step marked by a willingness to go wherever God calls.

Through every season, Lex has remained steadfast, contending in faith and placing his trust fully in Him. This book is a chronicle of that remarkable journey, a testimony of God's faithfulness and the power of a life yielded to His leading.

It is both inspiring and deeply encouraging, not only for believers but also for those who are still seeking. My prayer is that as you read these pages, you will incline your ear to hear what our Heavenly Father desires to speak to you through Lex's story."

Lim Geok Keng
Co-Founder of Châteaux

"I have had the privilege of knowing Lex for many years as a dear friend and brother in Christ. During our early years together in the same cell group, it was evident that he carried an unmistakable prophetic anointing. More importantly, what always stood out was his tender heart and sincere desire to please God in all that he did. His faith was never merely about spiritual experiences, but about wholehearted obedience to the Lord, even when the path was difficult.

Reading *What You Say, Daddy?* revealed a side of Lex that I had never fully known. While I witnessed his steadfast faith and the many testimonies of God's goodness, I was deeply moved by the struggles he quietly endured. It was heart-wrenching to read about those seasons, yet there was never any doubt that God had set him apart, not merely to overcome, but to walk in the fullness of the victory prepared for all who faithfully follow God.

Written with remarkable vulnerability and openness, this book is far more than a personal testimony. Inspired by the Holy Spirit, it beautifully unveils God's relentless love, faithfulness, and redeeming grace. Lex's story reminds us that even in our darkest moments, God never leaves us, never stops pursuing us, and is always working to fulfil His perfect purpose in our lives.

My prayer is that this book will encourage, strengthen, and draw every reader into a deeper relationship with the Father's heart. I wholeheartedly recommend it to anyone seeking to know God more intimately and experience the hope, healing, and victory found in Him."

Christopher Lim
Entrepreneur

"Some books leave you inspired. Others leave you with a deeper appreciation for who God is. As I read these pages, I found myself returning to one simple truth again and again: God is faithful.

What touched me most was not a story of an easy journey, but of a heart that continued to trust Jesus through every season. Through moments of joy and sorrow, certainty and waiting, personal trials and the call to serve others, God's faithful hand is evident throughout. Every chapter reflects His patient work of shaping character, deepening trust, and producing the precious oil that can only come through surrender.

More than a personal story, this book is a testimony of God's goodness. It reminds us that He never wastes a season. Even in the hidden places, He is at work, drawing us closer to Himself and transforming us into the likeness of Christ.

My prayer is that as you read, you will not simply admire the journey but encounter the faithfulness of God for yourself. May these pages encourage you to trust Him more deeply, surrender more fully, and find fresh hope in His unfailing love. Whatever season you find yourself in, may this testimony remind you that the God who has been faithful through every chapter of this story will be faithful in yours as well.

It is a gift that Lex has shared this journey so honestly. I pray it will strengthen your faith, draw you closer to Jesus, and leave you with a greater confidence in the One who is always faithful."

Rudy Taslim and Lam Bao Yan
Iris Living Oaks Singapore, Founders

"Some books tell a story; this one leaves a lasting imprint on the heart. Through profound brokenness, unexpected miracles, and unwavering faith, Lex Khoo beautifully reminds us that when we lean in and ask, *"What You Say, Daddy?"*, we encounter a Father whose voice is louder than fear, whose grace is greater than our failures, and whose faithfulness shines brightest in life's darkest moments."

Deborah Qiu, M.Div.
Pastor, Cornerstone Community Church, Singapore
Teaching and Curriculum Faculty, Global Awakening College of Ministry

"An honest and deeply personal testimony of God's unwavering faithfulness. Lex's journey so far—and the best is yet to come—is a powerful reminder that life is rarely straightforward. Unexpected challenges can arise without warning, doubts can creep in, and our faith can be tested. Yet our lives are not defined by the curve balls we face, but by how we respond to them. By a faith that continually looks upward to God, trusts Him in every season and is lived out daily with courage, hope, and unwavering dependence on Him."

Paul Choo (Boon Kim)
Chief Human Resources Officer
| Executive Committee Member | Board Director

"A heartfelt reminder that even in our darkest moments, God is at work, revealing His glory in ways we may not see or fully understand until we look back at the end of our journey. These powerful testimonies strengthen faith, rekindle hope, and beautifully reflect the unfailing love of God."

Soh Wai Leng

Pastor, Cornerstone Community Church, Singapore
Friend of Lex and Ginny

"*What You Say, Daddy?* is a book filled with the goodness of God. Lex's testimonies are evidence that he is truly sensitive to the voice of God and walks in obedience beyond mere human understanding and calculation. This has personally strengthened my faith walk, and I'm truly blessed!"

Senti Kevi

Co-Founder & Executive Director, Papa Foundation

"Lex's journey is one of learning to hear God, trust Him, and discover His ways. Throughout that journey, he experiences the goodness of God and learns that His ways are always better than his own. *What You Say, Daddy?* encourages us to embark on our own journey with Him with childlike curiosity. Thank you, Lex, for openly sharing your life with others."

Anthony Lee

Associate Director of TBH Consultancy
Devoted husband and a proud father of three sons

"This book is a beautiful and authentic testament to Father God's grace, faithfulness, and infinite love for His children. With honesty and tenderness, Lex pours out his life journey in Christ, always pointing gloriously to Jesus as his Anchor and Lord over all.

Whether in the quiet rhythms of everyday life or in defining, high-stakes moments, Lex's stories reveal a deep devotion and simple obedience to God. Readers will find themselves deeply encouraged and strengthened through these pages."

Winnie Tomlinson
Asst Pastor, Missions Coordinator,
Cornerstone Community Church, Singapore

"One concern I often have with autobiographical accounts is that they can sometimes reveal more than is good for the author, particularly when they are still active in the world. Yet, consistent with the way Lex has lived his life, he has chosen to lay it all out and let the chips fall where they may because of his trust in his Savior.

His transparency about his wounds and flaws will help more than a few readers identify with the dark times in their own lives, find comfort, and look heavenward.

Toni Morrison wrote, *"The function of freedom is to free someone else."* I think this is Lex's intent."

Freaderic Tan
A fellow sojourner and citizen

"Lex's story is a powerful testament to what it means to "Walk by faith and not by sight." A powerful journey of obedience, trust, and God's faithfulness."

Sharon Chong
Founder of Exodus 31 Design Pte Ltd / Prop Investment LLP

"*What You Say, Daddy?* is a profoundly touching testament of a true child of God living with deep faith, surrender, and intimacy with God even in life's most challenging situations.

I have personally known the author, Lex Khoo, for many years and have witnessed his life lived for the glory of God. Many tears are wiped away, hungry children are fed, and displaced people are restored through him and his household. From his journey of brokenness and pain, he turned to God and became a wonderful instrument of restoration to many, both far and near.

Miracles often come where there are challenges, restoration comes after brokenness, and the most radiant light comes after the darkest hour. This book reflects these truths and gently leads readers to our Daddy God.

Through his personal encounters and life testimonies, the author carefully leads readers to our Heavenly Father, who alone is the Anchor and Hope of our lives. This book encourages readers to journey through life with clearer vision, hope, and unceasing prayer to God, reminding us that the highest value of life is living for God."

Pastor Suluveyi Rhakho, PhD
Director, Harvest Ministries International

"*What You Say, Daddy?* was birthed when a simple everyday question between a father and his child turned into a powerful, revelatory God-moment. Lex's unreserved sharing evinces that life as a Christian is not a walk in the park, but is often inundated by the unexpected storms of reality. Yet his story testifies that as children of God, we can navigate through life's unpredictable and difficult curveballs by listening to God's voice and responding with obedience.

This book is easy to read and refreshingly inspirational. Beyond that, I believe God intends this book to be life-changing—bringing us into the tangible presence of God through the voice of our Heavenly Father, where the ordinary meets the extraordinary, and the impossible becomes possible.

Read and be immensely blessed!"

Dr Jane Yong
Fellow Sister in Christ
MBBS (Singapore)
MDiv (Trinity Theological College, Singapore)

WHAT YOU SAY, DADDY?

WHAT YOU SAY, DADDY?

HIS GLORY REVEALED IN THE DARK

LEX KHOO

ISBN: 978-981-94-6703-7 (Paperback)

ISBN: 978-981-94-6763-1 (Hardcover)

ISBN: 978-981-94-6704-4 (eBook)

Unless otherwise indicated, certain names and identifying details have been changed to protect the privacy of individuals.

First Edition 2026

CONTENTS

FOREWORD

I had not known, up till the point of reading the manuscript, of the amazing grace of God upon Lex. Above all that Lex is, he is a man who pursues after God. From almost ending his life, not once, but twice, to being an overcomer in life, Lex's life describes well the divine providence over his life.

The U-turn, of course, was his amazing encounter with Jesus. *What You Say, Daddy?* is a well-thought-out book that chronicles the adventure of a man who loves his God and seeks to walk with Him. The phrase *"What You Say, Daddy?"* is a heartfelt term of endearment and that's essentially how the Heavenly Father seeks to interact with all of us, with familiarity, yet with reverence. The one thing that has always struck me about Lex is his passion for His Master. He was a little different. He had his head in the clouds but his feet on the earth. And he has a strong prophetic disposition. This book is inundated with dabs of the prophetic. It is easy to read, captivating and it will challenge some of our presuppositions. Be blessed as you read it.

— Pastor Yang Tuck Yoong

Senior Pastor
Cornerstone Community Church

DEDICATION

For my beloved family.

For my parents and parents-in-law, whose love and sacrifices became stepping stones for the generations that follow.

For my beloved wife, Ginny, my companion through storms and sunshine, valleys and mountaintops, as we journey together through the great adventure of faith.

For James, Paul, and Hezekiah—may you grow to become men after God's own heart, deepen your intimacy with Christ, hear and obey His voice, and walk courageously in His ways.

For Gloria and Stellar, whom I await with joyful hope, until the day we are reunited beyond the veil of this life.

And above all, to my Lord Jesus Christ, my Heavenly Father, and the Holy Spirit.

Every page, every testimony, every victory, and every breath—all glory belongs to You.

ACKNOWLEDGMENTS

I am deeply grateful to the many pastors, leaders, and mentors whom God has placed in my life. Thank you for believing in me, encouraging me, correcting me, and helping me become more than I could have become on my own. Many of the lessons, testimonies, and insights shared in these pages were shaped through your love, guidance, and investment over the years.

To my dear brothers and sisters who have journeyed with me through different seasons of life, thank you for your prayers, friendship, and faithfulness. Your encouragement and support have been a constant blessing on this journey.

A special thank you to Anungla Longchari for your dedication and thoughtful expertise in helping edit this book. Thank you for helping bring clarity, structure, and refinement to these stories.

Most importantly, I thank my Lord Jesus Christ, my Heavenly Father, and the Holy Spirit. Thank You for carrying me through every valley and every mountaintop, and for revealing Your glory even in the darkest seasons of life.

Without You, I am nothing.

Every page, every testimony, every victory, and every breath—all glory belongs to You.

PREFACE

"What You Say, Daddy?"

My youngest son would lean in close, tilting his ear towards me and asking me to repeat what I had just said. It was not only the way he listened so intently, but the wholehearted readiness with which he received my words.

That simple moment became especially precious because it came after a season when he had begun speaking despite the odds. And in that moment, I began to see myself.

Leaning in to hear from my Lord; not only in everyday life, but especially through seasons of trial, desperation, and uncertainty.

His voice matters most.

Above every other voice.

Above every circumstance.

For His voice still calms the storms of life and brings victory in the face of overwhelming odds.

The Lord delights in using the least of the least to accomplish what seems impossible. I am one of them. Just another ordinary man with an extraordinary God; one whom the Lord lifted out of the miry clay, simply trying to follow His leading and obey Him, even while often wondering whether He should have chosen someone more capable and qualified instead.

In 2023, I sensed a strong impression from the Lord to

write this book. I had experienced similar thoughts before, but this time it felt different; clearer, weightier, and more certain. Though I was excited, I did not know where to begin or even what I was meant to write. Over time, the purpose became clear.

I wanted to write something that would honor my Lord and Savior, Jesus Christ, while also leaving behind my testimonies, life story, and lessons for my children. It matters deeply to me that they would see and know the Lord behind everything I am, because without Him, I am nothing.

I have always treasured testimonies. They have been a constant source of encouragement, not only to me but to many others as well. Testimonies are precious. Many are born out of sorrow, darkness, loss and wilderness seasons. Yet, as life moves forward and new stories emerge, old testimonies are often forgotten. But testimonies are not merely stories of the past. They carry a prophetic invitation—a reminder that what God has done before, He can do it again.

Revelation 19:10 (NKJV) says, *"For the testimony of Jesus is the spirit of prophecy."* Many times, I have asked the Lord to do in my life what He has done in the lives of others. He is a loving Father who knows what is best for each of us, and He is still willing to move powerfully on behalf of those who seek Him. So ask of Him. Trust Him. Believe that He hears you.

As it is written in James 4:2 (NKJV), *"Yet you do not have because you do not ask."* And in Matthew 7:7 (NKJV), *"Ask, and it will be given to you; seek, and you will find; knock, and it will be opened to you."*

As Papa Foundation began taking shape in 2024, my heart expanded even further. I felt led to write not only for my children and future generations, but also for those who may not have a father-figure in their lives; the orphaned, the forgotten, and those longing for a deeper relationship with their own fathers. It is my prayer that these stories will point you to Jesus and remind you that you are not alone in this journey. Life is not always easy. As you read on, you may discover that I, too, have walked through struggles, disappointments, and trials in different ways and measures. I hope these pages will bring you comfort, encouragement, and the strength to keep moving forward.

Our lives carry far greater meaning and purpose than we often realize. I remember how moved I would feel whenever I read about children suffering—especially those facing hunger, abandonment, and loss. Even in my younger years, I could never fully understand why it affected me so profoundly. Over time, however, I began to recognize that God had placed within me a portion of His heart for children, perhaps shaped in part through my own childhood experiences. I believe every child is wonderfully made and carries a unique God-given destiny (Psalm 139:14). It is not God's desire that any should perish, but that all would come to know Him.

There was also a season when I wrestled with how this book should be written. Should it openly reflect a Christian perspective? Or should it simply contain a father's advice so that more people might feel comfortable reading it? In the midst of that struggle, the Lord showed me something unforgettable.

I saw a vision of this book placed in a library in heaven, glowing with a warm light among many other books carrying the same radiance. In that moment, I knew this book was not meant merely for earthly encouragement, but to testify of Him for eternity.

So I chose to let go of my own concerns. I chose to be honest. Transparent. Authentic. And I asked the Lord that one day my children in heaven may read these stories and know the faithfulness of God through them. Now, I simply trust Him to bring the right message to every reader.

May you be blessed as you read this book. May the Lord speak into your circumstances and fill you with hope, peace, and life in abundance.

There is always hope in Jesus; for everyone. Yes, everyone, regardless of where you are or what you have been through. There is nothing too broken for Him to restore.

My life rests upon this truth:

"For with God nothing will be impossible."
Luke 1:37 (NKJV)

Be blessed.

INTRODUCTION

"Pray to God that He will hold back the rain, Heze."

One evening, the boys wanted to go to the beach at East Coast Park *to* play in the sea. Dark clouds had already begun gathering before we left home, and it looked as though rain would come at any moment.

Heze looked at me intently for a moment, then folded his hands and offered a simple prayer.

When we arrived, the dark clouds remained on the horizon, but the rain did not fall. The boys happily ran into the water while I stood nearby watching them play. It was one of those simple father-and-son moments that did not seem particularly extraordinary. Then something happened that I still struggle to fully explain today.

As I stood by the beach watching my children, I suddenly became aware of someone standing some distance to my right. After a short while, I sensed that person moving closer. Since there were many people around, I did not pay much attention at first. My focus remained on my boys, especially my youngest, who was not yet a confident swimmer.

The presence continued moving closer until it stood right beside me. It felt so tangible that it startled me. Out of the corner of my eye, I could see what appeared to be a white robe with gold trimmings. Somehow, I also sensed the person smiling gently while looking towards my children. The presence stood so close that I instinctively turned to look.

But there was no one there. No one across that stretch of beach.

The entire moment happened within seconds. Yet before I turned, there was already an overwhelming awareness within me; a strange mixture of familiarity and awe. The presence did not feel frightening. It felt deeply loving. Familiar. Safe. And deep in my heart, I knew it was Jesus.

Shortly after we left the beach, light rain finally began to fall. And even as I write this today, it still feels almost unbelievable. The experience was so tangible. So real. It was as though someone had been physically standing beside me, just like any ordinary person would.

That evening stayed with me because it reminded me of something simple yet profound: Jesus is nearer than we sometimes realize. Whatever situation you may be facing today, whatever season you may be walking through, He is right beside you.

Even when you cannot see Him.

Even when you do not feel Him.

Even when you may not know Him yet.

He is there.

Over the years, I have come to realize that some of the most life-changing moments with God happen in the ordinary moments of life. Not always during large gatherings, dramatic encounters, or mountaintop experiences. Sometimes He meets us quietly in the middle of confusion, desperation, disappointment, and unanswered questions. In a noisy world filled with opinions, fear, pressure, and uncertainty, I gradually learned that the most important voice to hear is His.

This book is ultimately not about an extraordinary man. It

is about an extraordinary God meeting an ordinary man like me.

Many times, I did not fully understand the seasons I was walking through. There were moments of darkness, struggle, uncertainty, and brokenness that felt overwhelming. There were seasons when I wrestled with questions internally while trying to keep moving forward externally. There were moments when life felt heavier than words could express. Yet through every season of my life, He has always been there.

Sometimes through quiet impressions and visions. Sometimes through Scripture. Sometimes through unexpected encounters. Sometimes through desperate prayers whispered on bent knees. And often, simply through learning to ask Him directly.

One recurring lesson I kept learning was this: Ask God what He is saying. Not merely what circumstances say. Not merely what fear says. Not merely what logic says. But what He says.

Learning to seek Him, wait on Him, and hear Him personally gradually became one of the greatest anchors of my life. Not perfectly. Not without mistakes. But progressively, through surrender, obedience, dependence, and even through moments of mystery that I could not fully understand. Perhaps that is why the phrase, *"What You Say, Daddy?"* became so meaningful to me. There is something deeply powerful about the posture of a child leaning in closely to hear his father's voice. Trusting. Depending. Listening attentively. Believing that what his father says matters more than the noise around him.

In many ways, I feel that this has also been my own spiritual journey with God. Learning to come before Him not merely with polished prayers or religious routines, but sometimes simply as a child asking: "*What You Say, Daddy?*"

This book was not written from a mountaintop experience. It was written through a journey of valleys and mountains: sometimes crawling through the mud, dust, and intense heat of life. It was written through real life. Through victories and failures. Through moments of faith and moments of wrestling. Through seasons of joy and seasons of tears. Through desperation, surrender, obedience, and repeatedly seeing God meet me there.

Some stories in this book still feel difficult for me to share openly. Some moments remain deeply personal. Yet I believe these stories were never meant to remain with me alone. Because testimonies are more than stories.

They are birthed through years of waiting, persevering, believing, and witnessing God bring His promises to pass. They are invitations for others to encounter His faithfulness, miracles, breakthroughs, and healing. And if God could meet me in my brokenness, He can meet you, too.

Perhaps you picked up this book while carrying silent disappointments, fears, weariness, or questions that no one else fully understands. Perhaps you are searching for direction. Or perhaps you simply want to know whether God is truly real and near. I pray that as you read these pages, you will discover for yourself that He is far nearer than you realize.

God has not forgotten you. He will never leave you nor forsake you.

More than anything, my prayer is that you will not simply remember my stories, but that through these stories, you will encounter Him for yourself.

May the Lord speak to you as you read this book.

May He bring hope where there is despair.

Light where there is darkness.

Peace where there is fear.

Clarity where there is confusion.

And direction where there is uncertainty.

I believe God wants to speak to you today.

So lean in and ask:

"What You Say, Daddy?"

CHAPTER 1

WHEN EVERYTHING BROKE, HE CAME

I took my remaining fifty dollars and went all in.

That afternoon, I stood there with the last of what I had in my hands; thin stacks of joss paper, bought with money that could have fed me for the next few days. But hunger was no longer my greatest concern. I needed a breakthrough. My family needed a breakthrough.

I placed each piece carefully into the fire, all the while hoping that heaven was witnessing my devotion and sincerity. My lips mumbled familiar prayers, but this time there was something different beneath them; something heavier, more desperate. When the flame touched the edge of the paper, it caught quickly. One sheet, then another, until the fire rose and consumed everything I had offered.

As the paper curled, darkened, and turned to ash, something within me was also crying out:

Surely this time it will work.

Surely this time heaven will see my devotion.

Surely this time something will change.

The smoke rose, thin at first, then thicker, carrying with it years of devotion, effort, and silent hope. I stood there longer than necessary, staring at the last flickers of flame. All that remained in my pocket was my bus card for the journey home.

I was desperate. My family needed a breakthrough. We had been fervent worshippers of our ancestors and deities for decades. Yet things had only deteriorated over the years, with no breakthrough in sight. I had tried my best to remember all the traditions and rituals; how each item should be placed on the altar and when the festivals should be observed.

Deep in my heart, I longed for a change. Surely the gods would see my devotion and effort. Surely my family would do better.

Growing up, I often heard stories about the entrepreneurial success of my grandfather. My father worked in the corporate world for a season before moving into business. He is an extremely hardworking man who, even today, rarely asks anyone for help. He relies almost entirely on himself.

But small businesses come with many challenges and uncertainties. There were seasons when we did not know whether we would have electricity or even running water. Most of our clothes were hand-me-downs from cousins and relatives, for which we were very thankful. They were usually still in good condition and often concealed the real struggles we were facing.

I remember failing all my subjects except for a marginal pass in Science in Primary Three. I still remember the disappointment on my parents' faces. They warned me that education was my only way out. Otherwise, I would end up doing the lowest-paying jobs possible, even in Singapore. I sat on the kitchen floor in semi-darkness, full of fear and self-reproach. Later, my father came over and offered a few comforting words. I knew I needed to find a way forward.

For months after that, I did almost nothing except study. Every single day, including weekends, I made myself go to the community centre study room, rain or shine. Gradually, things began to change. By Primary Six, I was top in my class and scored straight As for my PSLE.

Those years taught me that little help would come from others. I had to fight for myself and for my family. Hard work and self-reliance were the only ways I knew, alongside my devotion to the faith I had grown up with. But something never seemed to add up.

The level of devotion and intensity of worship never seemed to bring any tangible breakthrough to my family. We simply went through endless cycles where hardship felt more common than stability. I remember looking out of an airplane window one day at the vast clouds below, forming what looked like a beautiful heavenly landscape. Would this be where I would go when my time was up? Would I one day live amongst these clouds as a spiritual being?

I once asked an uncle about the chances of attaining such an ending. He told me the probability was like a turtle surfacing in a vast ocean and placing its head through a floating ring. The chances were almost impossible. It felt hopeless.

If that was the case, what chance did my family and I really have? I was told to do more good deeds to improve my chances. Deep within me, I wondered how many good deeds would ever be enough. Did I need to do better than the billions of people who had lived throughout human history in order to qualify? I never dared ask further. I simply kept those questions to myself. It felt hopeless.

On another occasion, I asked my grandmother whether she thought she would go to heaven. To my surprise, she told me she was not going to heaven but to hell. That, she said, was her destiny. I was astonished. This was a woman who had devoted decades of her life to worship and to helping countless people in need. Surely my grandmother would qualify?

As she continued explaining, I asked who then could enter heaven. She told me there were many more beings in the Western heavens than in the Eastern heavens, which she described as relatively sparse. That conversation left a deep impression on me as a young boy. I had no answers. I simply kept those thoughts in my heart. They were beyond my understanding.

In my younger days, I noticed that a particular group of people seemed happier. This is purely based on my own observations as a youth, but many of them appeared to belong to a different faith—generally Christians or those from the "Western" faith. I often wondered why they seemed so happy. Did they not face the same challenges in life; finances, family problems, academics, health issues, and everything else that comes with living in this world?

In my world, happiness felt difficult. Life often felt like a huge ocean trying to swallow me whole. All I could do was keep swimming and stay afloat. Yet I never seemed to find a shore on which I could rest. It felt like an endless cycle of staying afloat and sinking back into the dark waters. To me, these people seemed to be standing on an invisible boat. I knew some of them personally, and they had troubles, too. Yet they somehow managed to maintain a positive outlook without appearing to try very hard. As for me, I was simply trying to stay alive. Deep inside, I longed for rest, even a brief respite from the endless struggle.

A series of events hit me one after another. Family finances reached rock bottom. A relationship with someone I loved deeply came to an end. Student loans demanded repayment. I lost the desire to continue in my career at that time. Emotionally, I broke and sank deeper and deeper. No hope was in sight. A darkness came over me as I wrestled in my heart and mind with thoughts of ending it all. At one point, I broke.

I opened the window grilles, switched off the lights, and closed the door to the small room. I rehearsed the steps in my mind. How I would climb onto the railing. How I would jump headfirst. I needed to end the misery that felt as though it had followed me for most of my life. I was ready. I had gone through the scene countless times in my mind. In my heart, I had already said goodbye to my family. The world felt unfair. I no longer had the strength to carry on.

I was ready to jump.

REFLECTION

LOOKING BACK

Have you ever reached a point where life felt heavier than you could carry on your own?

A DEEPER QUESTION

When life strips away success, money, relationships, and certainty, what remains as the foundation or anchor of your life?

WHAT YOU SAY, DADDY?

When everything fell apart, I discovered that God was not afraid of my toughest questions.

The next time life feels overwhelming, talk to Him honestly. Tell Him what worries you, frustrates you, or keeps you awake at night.

Then simply ask:

"Daddy, what are You saying about my challenging situation?"

His answer may not immediately change your circumstances, but it may change the way you see and understand them. Seeing things through His eyes is the beginning of finding hope.

PRAYER

Heavenly Father,

Life can sometimes feel overwhelming. There are situations I cannot control, questions I cannot answer, and burdens I cannot carry on my own.

Help me see that You are bigger than every challenge I face. When my own strength is not enough, remind me that I do not have to be my own Savior. I need You.

Whether I know You well or am only beginning to seek You, help me discover that You are not distant or merely an idea, but a loving Father who is real, present, and more than enough for me.

Open my eyes to see You for who You truly are and teach me to trust You more each day.

Amen.

CHAPTER 2

HE NEVER LEFT

Just at that moment, there was a faint knock on the door. I steadied myself and held on to my resolve. Yet the knocks kept coming. They were becoming distracting. Then I heard a key being inserted into the keyhole.

I briefly thought about stopping whoever was on the other side from coming in. But how was I supposed to stop them and jump at the same time? The door creaked open, and light poured into the tiny room. It was my mother.

She had "spoilt the ambience" for the jump. It is strange how mothers have that effect. Even in your weakest moments, when they step in, you instinctively pull yourself together and put on a stronger front. I sighed. The moment was gone.

I walked over to the open window and stared into the

dark neighborhood. My mother stood beside me. We remained silent for a long time. Eventually, she tried to comfort me. She shared how difficult life had been for her and how she had endured. She spoke about the struggles of many others as well. It was the same familiar story of struggle, survival, and hardship. To me, it only reinforced the thought that I was just another person in this world, one among millions carrying pain and disappointment. Regardless, it became yet another reminder of what I felt was failure.

I often found myself looking at the moon and stars; at the beach, and even in the forests while serving in the army; reflecting on life and wondering about the meaning of it all. Life never truly made sense to me. Yet nature always seemed to provide some measure of relief. Maybe one day I would find a way. Maybe one day I could be happier and enjoy a good life, too.

I was willing to work hard, but sometimes hard work alone seemed inadequate. There must be something more that I am missing. Everything eventually built up to the point where I spent days in my room, replaying the painful moments of my life.

I had worked hard with the dream of starting a family with my then-girlfriend. I had only recently begun working and was seeing limited success during the initial year. Financial difficulties continued to weigh on me as I realized I could not support a marriage in the near future. The pressures began affecting every part of my life. I became less effective at work. My confidence diminished. The dream of building a future together seemed increasingly impossible.

Without fully realizing it, I began sabotaging my own relationship. I would deliberately pick quarrels because I had already disqualified myself in my mind. I could not let go because my heart was full of love for her. Yet, unknowingly, I was trying to make her let go of me. It sounds foolish now, but I genuinely believed that if you loved someone, sometimes you had to let them go. That was my thinking then. I felt I could not provide a good future for her, and I convinced myself that letting her go was the loving thing to do.

When the relationship eventually ended, it was devastating. Not only had I lost someone I loved deeply, but I knew I had played a part in destroying what we had. Shortly afterwards, I learned that she was with someone else. She had found the love of her life. She had given her life to Jesus and was now with a fellow believer. I promised her that I would never contact her again. To me, it felt like the ending of all endings. Emotionally, there was nothing left. But in truth, my life was just beginning to change.

~

DURING THAT SEASON, a close friend invited me to a weekday church service. Ordinarily, I would never have gone. But in the depths of my sorrow, I felt I had nothing left to lose. After a brief moment of thought, I promised that I would go.

A few hours before the service, however, a sudden and intense headache came over me. The pain was so severe that I spent most of the time lying in bed. No medication seemed to help. Wave after wave of pain throbbed through my head until I no longer wanted to go anywhere. I even prepared a message to tell my friend that I could not make it. He would understand. It was a perfectly reasonable excuse. Yet the promise I had made kept coming back to me. I wanted to keep my word.

At the service, I did not pay much attention to what the guest pastor was saying. He was an energetic African pastor, full of passion as he shared. Meanwhile, I sat there emotionally numb in my depressed state. Then came the final worship session. I decided to use that moment to speak honestly to a God I did not know. I said: *"If You are real, show Yourself to me tonight, and I will follow You forever."* Nothing happened. I sensed nothing.

My friend drove me home afterwards and asked if he could pray for me before I got out of the car. I reluctantly agreed. After all, I had nothing to lose.

Back home, I wondered what the whole evening had been about. God had not shown up. But when I looked at the clock, it was not yet midnight, so I put the thought aside and returned to my misery.

Shortly before midnight, I went to take a shower. Then suddenly, my heart began beating rapidly. And a thought came to me: *He is here.*

My mood changed instantly. Somehow, I sensed Him pacing outside the shower door. All I could think was: *I am not ready. I need to finish quickly and meet Him.*

Even today, it amazes me how my mental and emotional state changed so suddenly when I sensed His presence; a God whom I had only just challenged to reveal Himself.

When I finally opened the door, a strange shyness came over me. Even as a grown man, I found myself lowering my head as I stepped out.

I looked around. He was not there. Then I looked at the clock. It was already five minutes past midnight.

For days afterwards, I continued to wonder if what I had experienced was real. Yet I knew that in the depth of my depression, that sudden shift in mood and those overwhelming thoughts had not come from me. I continued pondering the experience over the next few days.

Sunday arrived, and I wrestled with a question. Should I go to church as I had promised? Or had it simply been an unexplainable experience? In that struggle, I chose not to go. Then, the following Wednesday, I had a dream. In the dream, the sister of the friend who had brought me to church asked me gently: *"Why didn't you go?"* My friend stood quietly behind her.

Then came another dream. A great flood swept through my neighborhood. Everything was washed away. I was in a boat with another man, looking at the floodwaters. Even houses had disappeared beneath them. As the waters receded, I still found myself picking up artifacts from my former faith.

The dream left a deep impression on me. Convicted, I went to church the following Sunday and gave my life to Jesus. Just when I thought my life was ending, a new beginning had begun.

I had thought that this was the moment Jesus and I became connected. But I was wrong.

When I was five years old, I attempted to slash my wrist with my grandfather's shaving blade. The truth is, I had learned it from a television show. I was deeply wounded by the domestic violence and constant fights between my parents.

I remember one particular incident when I stood right between them. They seemed like giants before me, shouting at one another. I was so frightened that I wet my pajamas. Witnessing those fights filled me with fear. The emotional pain felt too heavy to bear, and so I decided to end my pain.

Hiding in a room in my grandfather's house, I held the blade and cried uncontrollably. Part of me wanted to do it quickly. Yet at the same time, I was overwhelmed with emotion, sobbing at the thought of ending it all. What did ending even mean?

Then something happened.

A multicolored substance suddenly enveloped me. It resembled a foamy bubble flowing gently around me. Golden sparkles of light moved within it, shimmering through a clear, iridescent substance that reflected a spectrum of colors whenever light touched it, much like the surface of a giant soap bubble. In that moment, it felt as though time had stopped.

And there was a Man with me. He comforted me. I felt a sense of comfort unlike anything I had ever experienced before. My overwhelming emotions quickly settled as I listened to Him and experienced His presence.

As this happened many decades ago, I cannot remember exactly what He said. But I remember hope. I remember feeling that things would somehow turn around. And I remember feeling that I was no longer alone. I had felt so helpless. So abandoned. Yet He was there.

When I finally calmed down and decided not to go through with it, the substance and His presence slowly moved away.

For years, I never understood who that Person was, but I remained deeply thankful for the encounter.

Only after I came to know the Lord did I recognize that same voice, peace, and presence. It was Jesus.

"Before I formed you in the womb I knew you." (Jeremiah 1:5, NKJV)

He knew me long before I knew Him.

He came for me before I even knew His name.

He loved me before I ever thought of Him.

In my late teenage years, I responded to a salvation call by a senior pastor at a church service that a friend invited me to. I found the courage to raise my hand, pray the sinner's prayer, and go to the altar. Yet no one followed up with me afterwards, and even my friend thought I did not fully understand what had happened. Still, I remember a genuine sense of conviction in that moment.

Afterwards, I drifted into a kind of wilderness, returning to my old ways because I did not truly grasp what had taken place. That journey eventually led me to my breaking point—and to the moment when He met me again, as I shared earlier.

He never left. He never abandoned me.

"I will never leave you nor forsake you." (Hebrews 13:5, NKJV)

And He was about to transform my life.

REFLECTION

LOOKING BACK

Have you ever wondered whether there might have been moments in your life when God was watching over you, protecting you, or guiding you—even though you did not realize it at the time?

~

A DEEPER QUESTION

If God has loved you from the very beginning and has never stopped pursuing you, how might that change the way you see yourself and your life story?

~

WHAT YOU SAY, DADDY?

God had been present long before you noticed Him.

The next time you find yourself reflecting on your life, ask:

"Daddy, where have You been in my story?"

You may begin to see His fingerprints and presence in situations that you once thought were random. He has always been with you.

~

PRAYER

Heavenly Father,

Thank You that You loved me long before I first knew You. Thank You that Your love for me has never depended on how well I understand You or how close I feel to You.

Help me know You more deeply. Open my eyes to see that You have been with me all along—through the valleys and on the mountaintops, through moments of joy and seasons of struggle.

Forgive me for the times I failed to recognize Your presence or missed what You were doing in my life. Help me see my story through Your eyes and recognize Your faithfulness more clearly.

Draw me closer to You. Not simply to know more about You, but to know You personally as my loving Father.

Thank You that You never leave me, never give up on me, and never stop pursuing me.

Amen.

CHAPTER 3

THE GOODNESS OF GOD

Before my wife came into the picture, my life had already been going through a deep reshaping.

After I came to Christ, I left my job and began searching for work. It was a very difficult season. I was down to my last three hundred dollars, and I still had bills and installments to pay. On the outside, I tried to carry on normally. I still attended cell group, accepted invitations from friends, and tried to keep moving forward. But inside, there was a very real desperation. I found myself asking, *"God, are You going to help me? Is anyone going to help me?"* I needed provision. I needed direction. I needed mercy.

By God's grace, two job offers came quickly: one from a bank and another from a finance company. Logically, everyone around me would have chosen the bank. A friend in the financial sector told me plainly, *"Just choose the bank. It is an established, full-fledged bank."* Honestly, that made sense. But I was still learning how to discern God's leading. As I prayed, I sensed strongly that I should choose the finance company. It did not make logical sense to me, but inwardly I felt it clearly.

I still remember sitting in my room and speaking to this God whom I was only beginning to know. *"God, I am not familiar with Your ways yet. But if this is really where You want me to go, then I will choose the finance company. For better or worse, I will choose what I believe is Your choice."* So I did.

When I was posted to a branch, it turned out to be in Geylang. I remember arriving and seeing the atmosphere of the red-light district around me; the ladies walking up and down the streets, the older men lingering nearby, and the general environment surrounding the branch. Then I stepped inside and discovered another challenge. There were hardly any customers.

Some days, fewer than ten people walked into the branch, yet I was being measured on daily sales performance. I was still learning the products and trying to understand the job. To make matters worse, the location did not seem particularly suitable for investment-related work. Yet the branch manager was a Christian woman full of faith. She encouraged me often and reminded me to trust God. Sometimes she would pray short prayers with me, asking the Lord to provide and help us do well. I still remember how God began meeting me there.

Sometimes the counter staff would help introduce customers to me. One colleague once told me about a customer they had approached many times before, but she had never been willing to listen. Yet on that occasion, for some reason, she became open. By God's grace, we closed the deal. And it was not just once. It happened repeatedly in different ways.

My routine soon became this: whenever anxiety rose because hardly anyone had come in and I had not made a sale, I would go into the branch's handicap toilet, kneel down, and ask God for help. God answered those prayers. Week after week, He showed me His goodness.

Every Friday at cell group, I seemed to have another testimony. *"I have a testimony,"* I would say. *"God provided again."* That became part of my life; seeing the Lord meet me in my need and prove Himself faithful in situations that seemed impossible.

Later, I discovered that Geylang was one of the most difficult branches in which to perform. My sales manager told me that he did not expect me to survive there for long, but somehow, I thrived.

Eventually, I was transferred to better-performing branches and was given responsibility for two branches, including one in Serangoon. I did not know it then, but God was quietly arranging something that would alter the course of my life.

One day, a kind lady came into the branch and we began talking. Interestingly, for almost an hour we spoke very little about investments. Instead, we talked about Christian matters. She shared about her life, her children, and her faith. It was simply a good conversation. At one point, she mentioned that she had a daughter who was very active in church. Eventually, she decided to place an investment, and I helped her with it.

Some time later, she returned to the branch with two younger ladies. One was her daughter. The other was her daughter's friend. I greeted them in the usual way, and one of them was introduced as Ginny. That brief introduction led to an experience I will never forget.

As they were leaving the branch, I suddenly heard a voice. *"What do you think of her?"* The words were so clear and audible that I instinctively looked around. Who said that?

The lady, with her daughter Ginny and her friend, had just left the bank after a brief introduction.

The voice sounded as though someone had leaned in and spoken directly beside me; clear, steady, unmistakable, carrying both authority and love.

I looked around the branch. No one seemed to have heard anything. Everyone was focused on their work. Papers were moving. Quiet conversations continued. The normal rhythm of the branch carried on as though nothing unusual had happened. But inside me, something had shifted. Because I knew. It was the Lord.

This was not merely a passing thought. I was so stunned that I hardly knew how to respond. In fact, it took me more than half a day before I finally replied to Him.

It was the first time I had heard Him audibly, and a deep sense of awe settled over me. This was also my first encounter with Ginny. Ironically, I was so shaken by the experience that I could barely remember what she looked like, apart from her wind-swept fringe.

Who was this lady that the Lord would speak to me about?

I still remember the second time I saw Ginny. It was at Bugis, where we met because my former manager had arranged for us to get together. From a distance, I thought to myself, *Oh, is that her?* Then another thought crossed my mind: *She looks shorter than I remembered.* She also looked a little unwell and seemed rather pale.

The truth is, I had very little recollection of our first meeting. Later, I learned that she had indeed not been feeling well that day. Although we had already met once, this felt like our first real conversation.

We sat down at a restaurant together, but before long, my former manager suddenly announced that she had some urgent work to attend to and needed to return to the office. She left almost immediately. Just like that, the person who had arranged the meeting disappeared, leaving the two of us sitting across from each other, trying to make conversation.

It was slightly awkward at first. We were still getting to know each other, and I kept wondering when my former manager would return. But knowing her, I knew that once she became absorbed in her work, she would give it her full attention. Sure enough, she only reappeared much later, said she was not hungry, and then left again.

Since we still had time on our hands, Ginny and I decided to take a walk. Eventually, we made our way to Suntec City.

I still remember standing together at the rooftop area, looking out at the musical fountain. In that moment, I sensed something unusual. It felt as though I could sense the face of the Lord towards my right.

I could not explain it clearly then, especially because I was only about a year old in my faith. But I remember feeling that the Lord was looking at us and smiling. There was a quiet sense of approval. That was the beginning. The first semi-date, if I can call it that.

What struck me even more in those early days was how down-to-earth Ginny was. Before knowing the Lord, and especially as working adults, going out usually meant nicer places and more polished settings. But one of the places we visited was simply a hawker centre. It was hot, humid, crowded, and ordinary. We sat, ate, talked, and left. Yet I remember being quietly impressed. She was comfortable with simplicity. She was grounded. Something in me felt that this kind of person would fit not only who I was, but also whatever destiny God had for me.

After we had gone out a few times, she asked me a very direct question. *"Why are we always going out? What exactly are we trying to do here? If nothing is happening, perhaps we should stop going out."*

I appreciated that. She was not playing games. She wanted clarity.

By then, with many confirmations building in my heart, I felt that she was the one. The interesting thing was that before meeting Ginny, I had been enjoying my singlehood.

After coming to Christ, I felt free in a new way. I could spend time with the Lord, go where I wanted, take care of myself, and not carry the responsibilities that came with a relationship. I talked to God constantly during those days. I did not always hear Him, but I believed He was listening.

I remember being inspired by the parable of the persistent widow and deciding that I would be persistent, too. Even if I spoke ten thousand words to Him and He replied with just one, that was enough for me. I would keep talking.

So when the possibility of marriage appeared so soon, a small part of me felt slightly disappointed. This newfound season of single-hood seemed very short. Yet I believed His timing was perfect.

Before meeting Ginny, while still very young in my faith, I

had spent time getting to know a very nice lady who worked as a flight attendant. Despite our efforts, the journey never seemed to carry the Lord's blessing. After several months, I concluded that we were unequally yoked and decided not to pursue the relationship further.

It was not an easy decision. I explained that being different in faith would not work for me. She did mention becoming a believer, but something never sat right within me. I felt she needed her own conviction before God and not simply an added faith to make a relationship possible.

Looking back, I believe the Lord honored that decision. About a month later, Ginny came into my life.

At one point, someone advised me to make a list of qualities I wanted in a future wife. So I did. But as I looked at the list, I began asking myself a question: *If I truly trust God, why am I creating so many conditions? Why not trust Him more deeply?* Eventually, I reduced the entire list to one thing.

I had always been struck by the description of King David as a man after God's own heart. So I prayed: *"Lord, I want just one thing; a woman after Your own heart."*

I believed the heart mattered most. Someone who genuinely loved God would be a blessing to journey through life with. And as I got to know Ginny, I began to see that very quality in her.

When Ginny came into my life, I discovered that she was serving in the worship team, had recorded a song on a Christian album, and was far more spiritually mature than I was. That led to a different concern. How was I supposed to lead someone like this? I knew so little. She was already much deeper in ministry and in the things of God.

I still remember quietly talking to the Lord about this

concern one day outside the bank. Then He spoke to me again: *"I will lead you to lead her."* That settled something in me. If He was going to lead me, then my lack would not be the issue.

In my immaturity, I asked Him one more question. *"What if I don't choose her? Will You give me someone else?"*

The Lord replied very matter-of-factly: *"Yes, I will give you someone else."* I do not know why, but at that moment I suddenly pictured a buffet. I love buffets. There is always the best food, and then there is the rest.

I remember reasoning in my heart that if God is a good Father, then surely the person He had specifically pointed out must be His best for me. If I chose someone else, perhaps that person would still be wonderful, but I would always live with the question of what might have happened if I had trusted Him fully the first time. I knew I did not want to live with that mystery. So in my heart, I settled it. Ginny was my choice. When I shared my intentions with Ginny, she responded differently.

I was the sort of person who would say, *"Why not just ask God and let Him answer?"* Then we could move along quickly. But she was more thoughtful and measured. She needed time to process things with the Lord and allow Him to show her His will step by step. So over the next year, we both walked through the process seriously.

Every week, we attended two cell groups; hers and mine. There was no pressure, only a steady unfolding of God's will. At one point, I even went through an interview with her leaders. Two levels of leadership sat down with me at a restaurant and asked me questions. Afterwards, they sent me outside while they discussed the matter. Eventually, they called me back in and told me they were okay with us continuing our relationship. The remaining question was which church we would become part of.

Logically, it would have made more sense for me to join hers, since I was still so new in my own church. Yet in the end, Ginny came to mine. Not long afterwards, we were both being prepared for leadership.

I still remember my cell leader asking whether I would be willing to become a cell intern. He shared that there were others who knew much more than I did, people who were more knowledgeable in Scripture and more mature in the things of God. Yet somehow, they were not ready. As for me, I was barely more than a year into my faith. I honestly did not know if I was ready. But I had always wanted to help people. God had done so much for me; He had lifted me out of so much. Gratitude made me willing. So I said yes.

Ginny and I wanted to get married sooner, but we felt the Lord telling us to wait another year. So we obeyed. In total, we courted for almost three years before getting married. During that time, we also began looking for a home. The truth was that between the two of us, we only had about two thousand dollars.

God had been very good to me during that season. Within a year, I had paid off all my loans and had become one of the top salespeople in the finance company. I still remember writing a cheque to clear a large debt with one of my commission payments and thinking: *God, I cannot believe You have brought me here.*

Yet even after all that, we still did not have much money to begin married life. Still, we asked boldly. I even made a list of what I hoped for in a home; marble floors, certain features, and enough space for a future cell group. Looking back, it seems almost amusing. We had very little money, yet we were viewing homes and believing that somehow God would provide.

One day, Ginny's mother told us that a flat on the same floor as hers, directly across the corridor, was for sale. We went to view it. The moment I stepped inside, I was almost in shock. It matched so many of the things we had prayed for. Marble floors. A large enough living room for a cell group. Even the overall feel of the place seemed right. I told Ginny that we should go home and pray about it. So we did. But while praying, I felt a strong urgency to return immediately.

When we arrived, we discovered that another buyer had already made an offer and had gone to get the deposit. At that moment, something rose up within me. I simply knew: *This cannot be. This house is ours.*

I asked to speak to the owner and the agent. God had already placed a figure in my heart—$293,000. I did not negotiate. I simply offered that exact amount. It was only about a thousand dollars higher than the competing offer, yet somehow the owner paused, reconsidered, and eventually agreed to sell the flat to us and no one else. They could have started a bidding war. They could have waited for more offers. Instead, they chose us.

The next problem was that we did not have the deposit. I wrote the cheque anyway, even though the money was not there yet. Then we prayed. *"God, please provide. Let the cheque not bounce."* In His kindness, God moved my future mother-in-law's heart to help us. That was how we secured our first home in Serangoon. We were deeply thankful. It felt like a dream. This was the home where we would begin married life, prepare for our future, and eventually host our cell group.

Even our wedding became another testimony of God's provision. We did not have the resources for a large celebration. We did not hold a traditional Chinese wedding; only the church ceremony. Yet our cell group and church friends surrounded us with love. They helped with decorations, preparations, and countless practical needs. I felt strongly that we should invite everyone we could, because many of them might never otherwise step into a church. I also knew that I wanted to use the opportunity to share the gospel. So when I prepared my thank-you speech, it became something more than a thank-you speech. It was almost a mini-sermon, though without an altar call.

We invited over five hundred people, and more than four hundred attended, including many leaders and colleagues from work. I remember being nervous when I held the microphone. But once I began speaking, the words simply flowed. I shared from my heart about the goodness of God and what He had done in my life.

Meanwhile, downstairs, the catering was slightly delayed, and people were still scrambling to set everything up before the service ended. The truth was that we did not even know whether we had enough money to pay the caterer. So I asked my sister to take the *ang paos* (red envelopes of cash gifts) and count them at my mother's nearby flat while I waited and prayed.

When she returned with the total, it was more than enough. Not only was there enough to pay for the catering, but there was also enough for our honeymoon in Taiwan and for much of the furniture we needed for our new home. Once again, the Lord had provided beyond what we could imagine.

That was how we started. We began our marriage, our home, and our cell group carried by the goodness of God. The years that followed were filled with many more moments of His faithfulness; outreaches, Christmas gatherings, people coming to know Him, and eventually handing over the cell group to another brother in the group. But when I look back on that entire season, what stands out most is not simply that things worked out. It is that God came through repeatedly.

He lifted us.

He led us.

He provided when we had little.

He opened doors we could not open ourselves.

He made leaders out of people who were still learning how to follow Him.

If there is one thing I carry from that journey, it is this: The goodness of God is not an abstract idea. It is something I have seen in ordinary places; in awkward first meetings, in a handicap toilet where I prayed for sales, in a cheque that nearly bounced, in a home we could not afford, and in wedding bills we did not know how to pay.

His goodness met us not after we became strong, but while we were still weak and learning. Perhaps that is what makes His goodness so beautiful. It does not wait for us to become impressive. It meets us where we are and then, slowly and faithfully, carries us forward.

REFLECTION

LOOKING BACK

Have you ever experienced God's guidance or obey His leading in a way that made little sense at the time but later turned out to be a blessing?

A DEEPER QUESTION

If God's plans are truly better than your own, is there an area of your life that you still find difficult to trust Him with?

WHAT YOU SAY, DADDY?

God's goodness sometimes makes more sense looking backward than looking forward.

The next time you face a difficult decision, uncertainty, or change in plans, talk to Him honestly. Tell Him what you are hoping for, what concerns you, and what you do not understand.

Then simply ask:

"Daddy, what should I choose or do?"

His answer may not always be what you expect and often it will require faith to step into His direction. But knowing He is with you in obeying Him definitely helps.

PRAYER

Heavenly Father,

Thank You for Your goodness that anchors on who You are. So often I focus on what is missing and overlook the many ways You have already provided for me.

Help me trust You when I do not understand where You are leading. Help me trust not only Your hand, but also Your heart. Give me the courage to follow Your guidance even when it challenges my own plans and assumptions.

Teach me to recognize Your goodness not only in dramatic miracles but also in everyday moments of provision, protection, and grace.

Help me trust that You know what is best for me and that Your plans are rooted in love.

Amen.

CHAPTER 4

FROM MOURNING TO DANCING

I remember one scene very clearly. I was in the office toilet, inside a cubicle, feeling very low. Ginny and I had been married for more than four years, and we still could not have children. By then, it was no longer just a passing disappointment. It had become a silent ache that followed us from month to month and year to year.

I closed the cubicle door, knelt in that cramped space, lowered my head, and prayed. I asked God to help us have children. I remember reminding Him, almost childlike, about the visions and impressions of five children. If those really came from Him, then why had nothing happened for so long? Why had we tried everything and remained childless?

As I knelt there, I found myself repeating, *"God, give us a child. We will give our firstborn back to You."*

Somewhere in that moment, I felt something else I had not

expected; a strange sense of shame. Not because anyone had openly shamed us. But when you cannot have children for so long, something inside you begins to feel exposed. Everything else in life may seem to be functioning normally, yet this one area remains painfully empty. And you begin to wonder what is wrong.

That season was long and difficult. We did not sit back passively. We prayed. We asked our cell group to pray. We asked others to pray for us. At the same time, we did all the practical things as well. We went to doctors. We consulted Chinese physicians. We tried medications, tonics, and treatments that were meant to strengthen the body and improve our chances.

We kept going, hoping that perhaps the next step would be the one that changed something. But nothing happened. Month after month, there was no breakthrough. Over time, the question grew heavier. *Were we going to live the rest of our lives without children? What did this mean for us? What did this mean for all the promises and impressions we believed we had received from the Lord?*

Throughout those years, we were not alone. Many people in church knew of our desire for children and stood with us in prayer. Some shared testimonies that encouraged us. Others shared impressions and prophetic words they sensed from the Lord. One thing that was repeatedly spoken over us was that our first child would be a son.

Those words became precious during the difficult seasons. They did not remove the disappointment, but they helped sustain us whenever hope grew faint.

Eventually, we came to a point of surrender. I remember telling Ginny that perhaps we needed to stop trying so hard.

We had seen many doctors and taken many steps. While we were grateful for all the help we received, it felt as though striving had begun to take over our hearts. So we agreed to let go. We would stop seeing doctors for this. We would stop taking medications and tonics. We would simply rest in the Lord and trust Him. If children were going to come, they would come by His grace and in His timing. All the glory would belong to Him. There would be no doubt that it was the Lord who enabled us to have children. It was not a dramatic decision outwardly, but inwardly it was significant. We were no longer going to fight for this in our own strength. We would rest.

During this season, Ginny felt that the Lord was doing a work in her own heart. She had heard a sermon about having a good opinion of God. As she reflected on the years of waiting, she realized that her prayers had gradually become, "Why, God?" instead of "Thank You, God."

She recognized that she had become so focused on what we did not have that she had lost sight of His goodness. The message deeply impacted her. By faith, she chose to change the way she prayed. Instead of asking, "Why?", she began thanking God for the child she believed would come, trusting in His goodness even when His timing was different from ours.

Looking back, I believe the Lord was doing something deeper in both of us. He was not only preparing us to become parents. He was teaching us to trust Him and to hold on to a good opinion of Him, even in seasons when we did not understand His ways.

Around that time, there was a conference where a preacher shared that he had often seen miracles happen when praying for women who were barren. Ginny went forward for prayer. It was not long or dramatic; just a simple prayer. But afterwards, she sensed that something had shifted in the spiritual realm.

We went home and continued in that posture of rest. We were no longer striving. We were no longer trying every possible solution. We had given it fully to the Lord.

About a month later, we did what had become a familiar routine over the years: we used a pregnancy test kit. There had been many occasions before when nothing came of it. But this time was different.

I still remember the moment we realized Ginny was pregnant. I jumped out of bed in shock. I could hardly believe it. We had stopped everything. We were no longer striving. We had given it fully to God. And in that season of rest, James was conceived.

To us, it was a miracle. After more than four years of trying, praying, hoping, and facing disappointment, our firstborn came not during a season of striving, but during a season of surrender.

What made the timing even more unexpected was that shortly before that, we had felt repeatedly impressed by the Lord to join a trip to Honduras in Central America. After waiting for more than four years for a child, it seemed almost inconceivable to be making plans for such a long journey.

Close friends and family members were understandably concerned. They wondered whether it was wise for her to travel while pregnant. Yet both of us sensed assurance from the Lord when we prayed. Ginny felt assured that He would take care of both her and everything that is within her.

When we landed in Honduras, we had to travel through

the winding mountain roads, riddled with potholes and rough terrain. The bus bounced relentlessly, and with every jolt, my heart seemed to jump with it. Along with each bounce came waves of worry and anxiety. After waiting so many years for this child, I could not help but wonder whether the intensity of the journey might somehow harm our precious baby.

Yet in those moments, I kept reminding myself of God's promise and the assurance He had impressed upon us—that He would take care of everything within Ginny. Whenever fear tried to overwhelm me, I chose to hold on to His faithfulness. Looking back, I can see that the Lord was teaching me once again that the child He had given was also the child He was able to sustain and protect. James belonged first to Him before he belonged to us.

Throughout the trip, although a few others in the team fell sick, she remained well and James was protected. We returned safely to Singapore, grateful once again for the Lord's faithfulness.

YET THE STORY did not end there.

About twenty-three hours before James was delivered, Ginny suddenly started bleeding. The doctors informed us that the placenta appeared to be detaching from the uterine wall. If the condition worsened, the oxygen supply to the baby could be affected.

Naturally, we were concerned. After waiting so many years, this was the last thing we expected. Yet in the midst of it all, there was an unusual peace. We had prayed for this child for years. The Lord had spoken to us through many people, and His promises had sustained us through every disappointment. Friends and family stood with us in prayer, and somehow, peace carried us through those long hours.

Looking back, I realize that faith does not mean there are no difficult moments. It means knowing that even in uncertainty, the Lord remains faithful.

Twenty-three hours later, we finally held James in our arms.

The son that had been spoken of, prayed for, and waited for through more than four years had finally arrived.

He was more than our firstborn son. He was a reminder that the Lord had been faithful through every year of waiting, every disappointment, every prayer, and every tear. James truly was a miracle from a righteous God, given not because of our striving, but because of His grace.

Looking back now, I realize that through the years of waiting, the disappointments, the prayers, and the many decisions we had to make, God was doing a deeper work in both of us. He was not only preparing us to become parents, but shaping us to be the parents He desired us to be. Little did we know that this was only the beginning of another journey ahead, one that would require us to trust Him even more deeply and depend on His grace every step of the way.

Perhaps that was why, from the very beginning, we wanted to entrust even the naming of our children to the Lord. We did not want to simply choose names that sounded nice. We wanted their names to carry meaning and to remind us of what God had done.

So I prayed, and the name James came. For his Chinese name, I focused on the Chinese words of righteousness and miracle. In his case, those meanings were deeply fitting. He had come after such a long and barren season. To me, James was a miracle baby from a righteous God—a gracious gift that only the Lord could have given.

WHAT MADE the story even more remarkable was what happened afterwards. Less than a year later, Ginny conceived Paul. This time there was no striving, no struggle, and no long season of waiting. It was as though, after years of barrenness, she simply began to have children.

When Paul came, we prayed again for his name. I felt that his Chinese name should carry the meaning of abundance of grace. I still remember Ginny receiving the Chinese character *Hong*, and when we checked its meaning, it pointed to abundance. So, just as we had done with James, we prayed, sensed the name Paul, and gave it to him. But soon after Paul was born, the story took a very different turn.

Ginny was still recovering in the hospital when she began experiencing intense pain in her lower abdomen. The pain seemed especially severe whenever she needed to urinate. It became so unbearable that the doctors administered the strongest painkillers they could, yet they could not immediately determine the cause.

For days, her condition appeared to worsen. I remember watching her and feeling deeply alarmed. James was only about a year old at home. Paul had just been born. Yet my wife remained in the hospital, growing weaker while nobody seemed to know what was wrong.

I still remember driving one day with a terrible thought

pressing into my mind. *What if I lose her? What if this is the end?*

I began to cry as I drove and pleaded with the Lord not to take her away. *"Please, Lord, don't take her. The children need her. I need her."*

In my mind, I could already see flashes of what life might look like without her; raising two young boys alone and trying to cope without the woman I loved. I could not imagine it. That fear became one of the darkest moments of that season.

Eventually, after more scans and investigations, the doctors discovered the problem. There had been a cut in the bladder area. Urine was leaking where it should not have gone, causing immense pain and affecting the rest of her body. I remember feeling thankful that we finally knew the cause. Yet even then, the ordeal was not over.

Ginny had to undergo another operation. Afterwards, her body struggled to recover. Her intestines and internal organs had effectively gone to sleep because of the extensive internal wash that had been necessary. It took several more days before she could eat properly again and before her body slowly began to respond. Altogether, it was close to two weeks before she was well enough to return home to James and Paul. Those two weeks felt so much longer. I had never felt so relieved to finally bring her home to our two children.

That whole chapter of our lives carried both triumph and desperation. On one hand, James and Paul were clear signs of God's blessing and grace. On the other hand, the journey surrounding Paul's birth brought us frighteningly close to despair.

There were miracles. But there were also nights of great

uncertainty. There was rejoicing. But there was also pleading. That was the road we walked. Yet when I look back now, I still see the goodness of God all over it.

James came as a miracle in a season of surrender. Paul came as a sign of abundance after barrenness. And Ginny, though she endured such a painful and dangerous ordeal, came through it and returned home. We were left not only with two sons, but with a testimony that the Lord gives in His timing, sustains us in our weakness, and carries us through moments we never imagined we would overcome without His grace.

The years that followed were filled with the blessings of family life. We cared for James and Paul, brought them on family outings, learned the rhythms of parenting, and enjoyed the goodness of God during that season.

Looking back, I realize this chapter of our lives was not simply about finally having children. It was about learning that some things only come when striving ends and trust begins. It was about seeing that grace often arrives when we have exhausted our own strength. And it was about discovering that even after God gives, we still need Him every step of the way to sustain what He has placed in our hands.

As we looked back on those years, our hearts were filled with gratitude. We had witnessed His faithfulness through the waiting. We had seen His goodness in the victories He had given us. We rejoiced in His grace and were thankful for the lessons He had taught us about trusting Him and resting in His timing.

Little did we know that these precious experiences were the stepping stones onto a much deeper journey He had prepared for us. The Lord was about to lead us into a place where we would learn to trust Him even more, depend on Him more deeply, and discover dimensions of His love, faithfulness, and grace that we had never known before.

What we thought was the end of one journey was, in reality, only the beginning of another.

REFLECTION

LOOKING BACK

Is there an area of your life where you have been striving so hard that you have forgotten how to rest in Him?

A DEEPER QUESTION

Could it be that God is asking you to surrender something to Him rather than rely on your own strength for a breakthrough?

WHAT YOU SAY, DADDY?

Some breakthroughs come not through striving harder, but through surrendering more deeply.

The next time anxiety rises, tell God exactly what you are carrying. Tell Him what you are afraid of, what you are hoping for, and what feels beyond your control.

Then simply ask:

"Daddy, what should I do about this?"

If He wants you to surrender something to Him, lay it at His altar and rest in Him. That might just be the key to your breakthrough.

PRAYER

Heavenly Father,

Waiting can be painful. There are seasons when prayers seem unanswered and hopes appear deferred.

Help me trust You when Your timing differs from mine. Teach me to surrender what I cannot control and to place it into Your hands. Help me to stop striving in my own strength and learn to rest in You.

When I am weary, renew my strength. When disappointment has taken root, restore my hope. When fear has replaced trust, remind me that You remain faithful.

Thank You that Your grace often appears when my own strength has reached its limit. Help me see that You are still working, even when I cannot yet see the outcome.

Draw me closer to You through this season. Teach me to dwell not in my circumstances, but rest in Your goodness, Your faithfulness, and Your love.

Help me know You more deeply and trust that Your plans are good, Your timing is perfect, and Your grace is sufficient for me.

Amen.

CHAPTER 5

HOPE IN THE LORD

"*Daddy, remember last time you prayed for me that I could speak? Now I can speak."*

Hezekiah said it so simply, with such absolute conviction, that I was astonished by his declaration of faith.

He was six years old then, and we had been talking about something that required faith when suddenly, he said those words. It caught me completely off guard. Yet in that moment, something struck me deeply. He remembered the years we had prayed: *"God, please bless Hezekiah that he would be able to speak eloquently in multiple languages."*

More importantly, he knew. He knew it was God who had enabled him. He knew that God had given him that miracle.

Doctors had confirmed that Hezekiah was facing significant developmental challenges. He also had marked speech delays. Even when he was over three years old, we often could not understand what he was trying to say. He became frustrated easily and experienced frequent meltdowns. It often felt as though he was living in a world where no one understood him.

Long before Hezekiah was born, there had always been an impression in our hearts—both through our own prayers and through words shared by others—that Ginny and I would have five children. The first time we sensed it was while praying together before we were even married. We did not fully understand it, but the impression stayed with us.

After James and Paul were born, life settled into a rhythm. The four of us became a family unit, and over time the thought of having another child gradually faded into the background. It was no longer something we actively considered. Then, at a certain point, that impression resurfaced. It was as though the Lord was saying: *"It is time to have another child."*

We did not respond immediately. It took time to process. Three children would stretch us physically, emotionally, and financially. We knew that. Yet we also knew what we had sensed all those years. So after a season of wrestling and preparation, we chose to move forward in obedience.

I remember very clearly the moment I asked God for the name of this child. I was on the train, praying quietly, when the name *Hezekiah* appeared before me in an open vision. It was certainly not a name I would have chosen on my own. Yet it came clearly. At the same moment, I sensed the Lord saying: *"I will do something different."*

Along with those words came an understanding that this journey would be different from what we had experienced with James and Paul. I did not know what that meant. I simply took note of it and moved on.

When Hezekiah was born, we loved him deeply from the very beginning. He was a wonderful boy. But as he grew, it became clear that something was different. He struggled to speak. For the first few years of his life, he could not express himself clearly. As much as he tried, the words would not come out in a way that others could understand. He would repeat himself over and over, trying to be heard, until frustration eventually took over. Many times, we would look at one another and ask: *"Does anyone know what he is saying?"* And he would look back at us, confused as to why nobody understood him.

Experts told us that things would become more difficult as he grew older. They spoke of increasing frustration, more frequent meltdowns, and the need to prepare ourselves psychologically for a lifelong journey. We were also told that mainstream schools might not be an option for him.

I remember one day when he was still a baby. I carried him in my arms and tried to look closely into his face. I tilted my head towards him, hoping to catch his gaze. But he would not look directly at me. His eyes moved from side to side, but never met mine. Something about that moment unsettled me. It was subtle, but enough to raise a question in my heart: *Is there something wrong?* That was when the earlier words of the Lord came back to me: *"This will be different."*

Because Ginny worked in the special-needs field, she sensed that we needed a proper assessment. So we went to the hospital and consulted various specialists. As Hezekiah grew, it became increasingly clear that he faced significant developmental challenges. His speech, learning, communication, and overall development were delayed. The developmental challenges were significant enough that specialists and other professionals painted for us a bleak future—one we struggled to accept.

I still remember how much I dreaded those appointments. Every visit seemed to involve another long list of developmental milestones that Hezekiah had not yet reached.

As a parent, it felt overwhelming. At times, it seemed hopeless. There were moments when I broke down. I remember asking God, *"How are we going to do this?"*

How do we care for a child who needs support for the rest of our lives? My mind raced ahead to the future. I thought about finances, long-term care, and what would happen when we were no longer around. I even wondered whether our older boys would eventually have to carry that responsibility. Yet deep down, I knew this was ours to carry.

There was one moment I will never forget. We were on a cruise; just Ginny, Hezekiah, and me. I stood inside the cabin, facing the balcony and looking out at the sea, overwhelmed by everything. Hope and despair often come in waves that defy reason. There are moments when darkness descends so suddenly that, for a time, you lose sight of everything else. In those moments, it can feel as though there is no way forward. As I looked ahead, I could only imagine the rejection, pain, struggles, and difficulties Hezekiah might face in life. The despair was intense.

Thankfully, grace intervened. Instead, I held his hand and wept. Such a lovely boy from the Lord. Slowly, the ache in my heart eased. And I knew we had to continue this journey. He was my responsibility. He was my beloved son. I would walk with him for as long as I lived and trust the Lord with the rest of his story.

Over time, I grew frustrated with the medical process. One day, I told a doctor directly, *"We don't need you to keep telling us what he cannot do. We can already see that. What we need is help. What can we do for him?"*

After that, I shifted my focus. I chose to stop attending the review sessions with Ginny because I found that they were affecting my faith. The reviews were not helping me. Ultimately, only God could bring about the transformation we longed to see.

We remained grateful for the expertise and support of the professionals. But I realized that I was not looking merely for incremental improvement and lifelong coping strategies. I had seen healings, deliverances, and restorations before; both in my own life and in the lives of others. I could not believe that this would be the final conclusion for Hezekiah. He needed to be able to speak. He needed to communicate so that learning and development could flourish. I realized that I could not keep praying merely for a human outcome. I needed a Jesus outcome. Something beyond what human effort alone could accomplish.

To me, a miracle looked like this: One day, Hezekiah would stand on a stage and speak eloquently in multiple languages. Not merely speaking, but communicating with confidence, clarity, and influence. Like the Apostle Paul, speaking with wisdom and eloquence. That became my prayer. *"Lord, bless Hezekiah that he may speak eloquently in multiple languages."*

At the time, it sounded impossible. But I continued praying it with Hezekiah. Again and again. Some days with great faith. Other days with very little. But still I prayed. We asked others to pray. We laid hands on him. At that point, all we really had was God. If He did not come through for him, no one else could.

Slowly, we began to see small changes. The first time I heard him clearly say, *"Daddy,"* was one of the greatest joys I had experienced in a long time. We celebrated every little victory.

He attended a specialized preschool programme for a period of time. Later, the teachers recommended that we try placing him in a kindergarten where he could interact with children who were able to speak more fluently. They told us that he was the first student they had seen make such significant progress that they believed he would benefit more from a kindergarten environment.

Our search was not easy. We faced rejection after rejection. Some schools felt they were not equipped to support his needs. Others had previous experiences that had not worked out well for the rest of the students. But eventually, one kindergarten gave us a chance.

It was not easy. He had meltdowns, disrupted lessons, struggled to sit still, and found it difficult to adapt. Feedback came constantly. Over time, I learned not to absorb every negative report.

I remember one parent-teacher-principal meeting in particular. Ginny and I sat quietly as the teacher shared the immense challenges she was facing with Hezekiah. We felt genuinely apologetic. At that point, it seemed as though the only solution would be for him to leave the school. But the principal chose to stand with us. She simply said, *"Let's give him more time."* And from that low point, we began to see gradual improvement.

More recently, when Hezekiah was about six years old, further assessments gave us a deeper understanding of the specific developmental challenges he was facing. Although the news was difficult to receive, it also brought clarity. We now had a better understanding of how to seek the right help and support him. God faithfully provided the teachers, guidance, and resources we needed for that season, and we remain deeply grateful.

Along the way, He also brought the right people into our lives to support him. What has been especially encouraging is that even with these challenges, we continue to see growth. Week by week, there is progress. Sometimes it is very small; almost easy to miss. But it is there. And we have learned that while we should seek help and better understand the challenges he faces, we must also continue to pray and trust the Lord to help him overcome, even at such a young age.

There was another moment that anchored me deeply. I was in church during worship, and I told the Lord, *"I cannot walk this journey without knowing how his life will turn out."* God graciously responded by giving me a vision. I saw a skyscraper filled with people working. Then I saw an older man, perhaps in his sixties, seated at a large table, writing. I could not see his face clearly, as I was looking down at him from behind and his head was bowed. Yet somehow, I knew it was Hezekiah. And somehow, I knew that by that time I was no longer around.

God was showing me his future. In that vision, I knew he was doing well. I knew he was functioning independently. I even knew that he was a chairman. That was all. But it was enough.

From that day on, whenever doubt crept in, that vision became something I could hold on to. It seemed far removed from our present reality. But it was something God had shown me. And that mattered.

Today, Hezekiah still has challenges. There are still occasional meltdowns. There are still days when he becomes discouraged and doubts his own abilities; sinking in his own negative self-talk. When that happens, I look him in the eye and tell him, *"God has given you a good mind. You are growing. You will get better."* I repeat those words again and again. And sometimes I can see something settle within him. He is beginning to believe the truth being spoken over his life.

I believe God has given parents authority to speak life over their children. We can pray, take authority over situations, and declare God's truth over their lives. With God, nothing is impossible.

Now, Hezekiah speaks. A lot. Sometimes he speaks more than anyone else in the house. He asks questions. He engages in conversations. He shows love to people who visit our home. He is bold in his own way, unafraid to approach adults —even strangers he meets outside.

He has entered the primary school that we believe God showed us, with a godly form teacher whom we believe God has placed in his life. Even the school itself was part of God's plan, something we did not fully recognize until everything came together. Unlike the rejections we faced during our kindergarten search, God enabled him to enter this primary school in the first round of selections.

Today, some doctors have even begun to question whether

his earlier assessments were accurate. He has improved so much and achieved many milestones. To be honest, that matters less to me now. My eyes are on Jesus when it comes to Hezekiah. I have the vision of his future to hold on to. And I still believe that one day he will speak eloquently in multiple languages, in God's perfect timing. There is still a long way to go. But there is also so much to be thankful for. Hezekiah now enjoys Bible time during our family devotions. He may not understand everything, but he is interested. And that brings me great joy.

There was an ordinary day recently when I felt he was ready. I asked if he wanted to receive Jesus. He said yes. So we prayed together. The Lord's presence was so tangible, and we rejoiced with him. He knows that he is a child of God. He has also expressed a desire to be baptized, so we will wait until he reaches the minimum age required by our church. We look forward to that day.

When I look back, one thing stands out clearly. Do not lose hope. Even when things seem impossible. Even when reality feels heavy and suffocating. As parents, we must continue to speak life into our children. We must continue to believe, pray, and trust. In a sense, we can carry faith for them when they do not yet have the ability to believe for themselves. Because every child carries a destiny in God. We may not fully understand it, but in His time, it will unfold. Until then, we hold on. We keep speaking truth. And we do not lose hope.

REFLECTION

LOOKING BACK

Is there someone you love deeply whom you have been praying for, worrying about, or struggling to help?

A DEEPER QUESTION

When progress seems slow and circumstances remain unchanged, do you still persist in praying and believing in God's possibilities?

WHAT YOU SAY, DADDY?

Every child is unique. What others may see as a limitation, God may see as part of a greater story yet to unfold—that will echo for eternity.

The next time you are thinking about someone you care deeply for, talk to God about them. Tell Him your hopes and fears.

Then ask:

"Daddy, show me the destiny and plans You have for him/her."

And don't be afraid to pray boldly. Declare God's promises. Pray "impossible prayers", knowing that nothing is impossible with Him.

PRAYER

Heavenly Father,

Thank You for the people You have entrusted to my care and love.

When I become discouraged, help me remember that nothing is impossible for You. Teach me not to measure a person's future by what I see today, but by who You are.

Help me trust that every child is wonderfully made in Your image, with a purpose and destiny known by You. Remind me that every person's journey is different, and that what may seem like a limitation today may one day become part of the very thing that makes them unique.

Give me patience when progress seems slow, faith when answers seem delayed, and wisdom to love well through every season.

Help me persevere in prayer and not lose hope. When I am tempted to compare, remind me that You are writing a different story for every life. Teach me to trust Your plans, Your timing, and Your faithfulness.

Above all, help me see this person through Your eyes and love them as You do.

Amen.

CHAPTER 6

GLORIA – THE LOVE I NEVER GOT TO HOLD

Before I had any children, I had a vivid dream. In the dream, five children were playing in the living room of my first matrimonial home with Ginny. They were running around, making a lot of noise, and I remember telling them to stand in a line while I lectured them. I saw three boys and two girls.

That dream stayed with me through the many years that followed; through joys and heartaches I could never have imagined. It was also the first time I saw Gloria and Stellar, my two lovely daughters.

Years later, I had another vivid dream involving Gloria. She appeared to be about four or five years old and was playing in front of a dressing table with some cosmetics. There was a special atmosphere around her, almost as though a liquid substance filled the room, carrying golden sparkles within it. I was casually talking to her as she played.

What stood out to me was the dressing table. It was unusual in design, with three mirrors, two of which opened outwards to the left and right. In that dream, I sensed the Lord saying only one thing: *She is beautiful.*

Many years later, Ginny and I were in a furniture shop when I suddenly saw that exact dressing table. It was unique in its design, and I recognized it immediately. I eventually bought it with my bonus payout as a gift for Ginny.

The name Gloria also came to both of us independently. At the time, I was in Mozambique on a mission trip. To this day, it remains one of the most impactful mission trips of my life. It also took place during a particularly difficult season. I was between jobs, and financially things were not easy. We had rented out our home and moved in with my mother-in-law. Even so, I felt strongly that the Lord wanted me to go on that mission trip.

Right up to the final days before departure, I wrestled with the decision. From a practical standpoint, it did not seem wise. But I have learned that when following the Lord, logic does not always have the final say. Very often, we only understand later why He asks us to do certain things.

During that trip, I spent much of my free time in a prayer hut where people prayed around the clock. I especially loved being there in the mornings. I would sit quietly with my Bible and simply soak in the atmosphere of prayer and worship.

One particular day, I lay down and looked up at the inside of the roof. Then something extraordinary happened. The heavens opened. I found myself looking into what seemed like heaven itself. What I saw was an indescribably beautiful garden filled with lush greenery. There were animals unlike anything I had ever seen before, though some resembled animals on earth. I remember one that looked somewhat like a deer. Yet everything was different. The colors were vivid and alive in a way that is difficult to describe. The trees and shrubs seemed to radiate life and beauty. Even the shades of green appeared brighter and more vibrant than anything I had ever seen. Everything was breathtaking.

As I looked on, I remember thinking about people who had spoken of visiting heaven and then returning to earth. In that moment, I understood why some of them had struggled to come back. The beauty was beyond anything I had ever known. Then the vision changed.

A baby girl wrapped in white linen descended through the roof and slowly moved towards me. Seconds later, she landed gently in my arms. At that very moment, I heard a voice from heaven say: *"Gloria."* I immediately took note of the name so that I would not forget it.

When I returned to Singapore, I asked Ginny whether the name Gloria meant anything to her. She paused for a moment and looked at me in amazement. Then she told me that she had written the same name in her journal. The Lord had spoken to her separately, but she had never mentioned it to me. It was a deeply special moment. We knew that God Himself had named our daughter.

When Ginny became pregnant after the birth of our three boys, I was overjoyed. Deep down, I had always believed that having a daughter would introduce me to another beautiful expression of love. After falling in love with Ginny, and raising our three sons together, I imagined that loving a daughter would be the closest thing to experiencing that wonder all over again. I could only thank God for the opportunity to fall in love one more time.

Life continued as usual with work, family, and ministry, while we attended regular appointments with the gynecologist. Throughout the first trimester, nothing seemed unusual. Each visit brought another opportunity to see Gloria on the screen and hear her heartbeat. By then, I had already seen her several times in dreams and visions. I was simply waiting for the day I could finally hold her in my arms. Although I rarely spoke about it openly, I was looking forward to her arrival immensely. I imagined the adventures we would have together as a family and all the precious moments that lay ahead. Then came the day that changed everything.

We arrived at the clinic for what we thought would be another routine check-up. As usual, I watched the screen. At first, nothing seemed wrong. But then I noticed a change in the doctor's tone. She continued searching for the heartbeat. Once. Twice. Several times. A sense of unease began rising within me. Was the machine malfunctioning? Was it simply difficult to detect the heartbeat that day? Yet with every unsuccessful attempt, my concern grew. Eventually, the doctor spoke the words I never expected to hear. Our daughter had passed away.

Nothing about it made sense to me. My thoughts spiraled immediately. Hadn't the Lord prompted us to try for another child after our three boys? Hadn't He shown us Gloria in dreams and visions? Why was this happening? My heart broke. I had lost my daughter. She had not even lived for three full months. We had only a short time between discovering her existence and losing her.

I could not comprehend what had happened. I remembered how, when Ginny was pregnant with James, we obeyed the Lord and went on a mission trip to Honduras. I remembered the promises and assurances He had given us during that season. So why this? Why Gloria? I did not know how we survived the shock. I did not know how we carried the grief. Why would God speak to us about Gloria and reveal so much about her if I would never have the opportunity to hold her in my arms? I felt lost.

Even after years of following the Lord, witnessing miracles, seeing God move in countless situations, and helping others navigate their own pain as a leader, I found myself without answers. Many things in life can be replaced or rebuilt after they are lost. This could not. This loss felt permanent for my time on earth. Grief gripped me deeply.

There were days when I lay on the floor for hours, soft worship music playing in the background, speaking to the Lord and simply sitting with the pain. The Lord gives. And the Lord takes away. All I had was those brief months of knowing she existed. Why couldn't she stay? Why couldn't I have more time with her? I never received a direct answer. Yet through it all, I always sensed that He was near.

I never blamed God for the loss. He is sovereign, and His wisdom is beyond mine. But grief does not disappear simply because we trust Him. It came in waves. Sometimes unexpectedly. Sometimes when I thought I was doing better.

In the midst of that grief, I began doing something unusual. I told the Holy Spirit that He could do anything. Then I asked Him for help. I would imagine myself sending voice messages to Gloria. I would speak to her as though she could hear me. I would tell the Holy Spirit, *"Please help me send this message to her."* Then I would share whatever was on my heart. When I finished, I would thank the Holy Spirit for delivering it. Perhaps it was my way of processing the loss. Perhaps it was my way of remaining connected to the daughter I never got to hold. But in my heart, I genuinely believed she received those messages.

Even now, years later, the memory of Gloria can still bring tears to my eyes. I do not believe time simply erases a loss like this. But time has softened the sharpness of the grief. And over the years, something else has grown within me. Hope. A determination to see my daughter again. As a believer, I know that this life is not the end of the story. Gloria is with the Lord. She is safe. She is loved. She is in good hands.

For now, my responsibility is here. I must take care of the family God has entrusted to me. I must continue to live faithfully, and finish the race He has given me to run. And one day, when my time on earth is complete, I will see her again. We will have eternity to catch up. I will tell her all the stories she never got to hear. And at last, I will hold my daughter close.

REFLECTION

LOOKING BACK

Is there someone you miss deeply or a loss that still brings tears to your eyes?

A DEEPER QUESTION

If this life is not the end of the story, how would you view temporal separation and loss of your loved ones?

WHAT YOU SAY, DADDY?

If there is someone you miss deeply, spend a quiet moment today talking honestly with God about that loss.

Then ask:

"Daddy, what would You like me to know about this temporal separation?"

You may still feel the pain of the loss, but your hope in His greater story of future reunion and eternal companionship will give you peace and hope.

PRAYER

Heavenly Father,

Thank You that nothing entrusted into Your hands is ever lost.

You know every grief I carry. You know the names, memories, hopes, and dreams connected to the losses I have experienced.

Some pain remains difficult to understand. Yet You invite me to bring all of it to You.

Thank You that You are near to the brokenhearted. Bring comfort where there is pain, peace where there is turmoil, and healing where there are wounds.

Help me trust that even when I cannot understand what has happened, You remain good, faithful, and loving. Help me believe that You can redeem every tear, every loss, and every disappointment for purposes greater than I can presently see.

Teach me to see this part of my story through Your eyes and to rest in the assurance that Your love never fails.

Amen.

CHAPTER 7

WHEN ANSWERS NEVER CAME

The impression from the Lord came again. *Try again.* Really? I was still recovering from the loss of Gloria. What would Ginny think? She might not agree to trying again at this stage. We already had three boys, and our hands were more than full. Yet the impression remained. What about the sense that we would have five children? What about obedience to God? Perhaps this time we would finally have a daughter.

I told the Lord, *"You will have to speak to Ginny Yourself and convince her. She needs to hear from You on her own. I will tell her what I sense, but she must hear from You, too."* The impression remained clear.

Ginny was not keen to try again, at least not so soon. Only a few months had passed since Gloria's miscarriage. I understood her hesitation. After three difficult pregnancies and one miscarriage, she had already been through so much. Yet there seemed to be a sense of urgency. It felt as though there was a window of time in which we were meant to try.

After many weeks of wrestling and prayer, we finally came to a place where we chose to obey and trust the Lord. Soon afterwards, Ginny became pregnant. And so we found ourselves back at the same clinic, with the same gynecologist, going through the same process once again.

Every visit brought back memories of Gloria. Yet hope remained. Maybe this time things would be different. Maybe this time I would finally have a daughter to hold. Maybe this time I would experience that special love I had always imagined. There was still sadness from Gloria's loss. But there was also anticipation.

As we always did, we prayed for a name. When the name Stellar came to me, it felt clear. Ginny considered a few other possibilities, but we both commit to the Lord's choice.

The pregnancy progressed under careful medical supervision. Our gynecologist took every precaution possible. Even so, every scan felt different after what had happened with Gloria. We held our breath each time.

Towards the end of the first trimester, we went for another routine scan. I sat quietly on the bench as the examination began. Everything seemed normal. I was already imagining the future. The boys would finally have a sister. I thought about the clothes I would buy for her. The places I would bring her. The photographs we would take together. All seemed well. Then I noticed the doctor becoming quieter. She adjusted the machine. She tried another angle. Then another.

Then she restarted the equipment. My heart began to sink. Surely not again. The memory of Gloria came rushing back. *Please, Lord. Not again. We obeyed. You told us to try. Surely Stellar will be alright.* My mind was racing. Then the words came. "*She is gone.*"

Tears streamed down my face. I wanted to run out of the clinic. How could this happen again? We asked the doctor what had happened. She explained every possible medical reason. Yet none of the explanations helped me understand what God was doing. Earlier, we had requested a test to determine the baby's gender. The results confirmed what I had already seen through dreams and impressions. She was a girl. She was Stellar.

I do not know how we held ourselves together that day. We sat outside the clinic, devastated. Neither of us had answers. We asked each other questions. We asked God questions. But everything remained a mystery. This was our last opportunity. Ginny had reached an age where another pregnancy would not be advisable. And so the reality settled upon us. We truly did have five children. Three boys. And two daughters. The difference was that I would only get to hold my daughters in heaven.

I tried to process everything logically. If we had not obeyed and tried again, Gloria and Stellar would never have existed. Although we lost them on earth, we had not lost them forever. We would have eternity together. For now, they would simply not be part of our earthly journey. Thirty years. Forty years. Fifty years. Compared to eternity, it would only be a moment.

God has His reasons. God has His purposes. At least, that

was what I kept telling myself. But grief is not easily overcome by logic. The sorrow ran much deeper. For a season, I simply sat in the darkness of it. The Lord had told us to try twice. Twice we obeyed. Twice He gave. And twice He took away.

I searched for explanations. I revisited every impression, every dream, every word. Yet nothing connected in a way that provided a final answer. This became another mystery that I believe I will only fully understand in heaven.

For a season, I continued to "send" voice messages to Gloria and Stellar through the Holy Spirit. It may sound unusual, but it became one of the ways I processed my grief. I would speak to them from my heart and ask the Holy Spirit to deliver the message. Whether others understand it or not, more importantly, it brought me comfort.

During Ginny's pregnancy with Stellar, I had a vision of Gloria in heaven. In the vision, she was alone and seemed sad because Stellar was no longer with her. Prior to that, I had always sensed the two of them together and very close to one another. At one point, a thought crossed my mind that perhaps Stellar had chosen to return to Gloria because of that closeness. Of course, I cannot say this with certainty. It remains only a personal impression.

I remember one day while riding in a taxi, the Holy Spirit gently asked me why I had stopped sending them voice messages. I had stopped for a while because part of me was trying to reconcile the facts, make sense of everything, and move on. Yet even in that season, the Lord remained close. Over time, I learned to live with mysteries. Not every question receives an answer in this life. Not every sorrow comes with an explanation. Sometimes trust must exist where understanding does not.

There is no bitterness in my heart towards God. We are all stewards of whatever He entrusts to us, and that includes our children. For a season, Gloria and Stellar were entrusted to us. Now they are with Him. And they are in far better hands than ours. Meanwhile, we still have a life to live, challenges to overcome, and three wonderful boys to raise. My daughters are safe with the Lord. That gives me peace.

The Lord also gave encouragement to our family in unexpected ways. Paul once shared a dream in which he saw Gloria and Stellar together in a photo frame. That was how he knew how Stellar looked like. The boys were saddened by the loss of their sisters, and in their own way, they grieved, too. God's grace carried all of us through that season. Even now, we continue to hold Gloria and Stellar close in our hearts. Similarly, Ginny had a vision of both Gloria and Stellar during an altar call at church. Moments like these became reminders that they were real, that they mattered, and that God had not forgotten them. To us, they were never merely pregnancies. They were our daughters.

As I reflect on it all, I still do not have all the answers. I do not fully understand why the Lord asked us to try again. I do not fully understand why He gave us two daughters only to take them home so quickly. Perhaps those answers will come one day. Perhaps they belong to eternity. But this much I know: God is good. God is faithful. And God can be trusted, even when we do not understand His ways.

We love the Lord.

We have learned to fellowship, in some measure, in His

sufferings. And we believe that He has good plans for us. One day, everything will make sense. Until then, we will continue to trust Him. And when our earthly journey is complete, our family will be whole again. On that day, I will finally meet Gloria and Stellar face to face. And I will hold my daughters for the very first time.

REFLECTION

LOOKING BACK

Have you ever found yourself disappointed with God because life unfolded differently than you expected?

A DEEPER QUESTION

If God never fully explained the "why," would you still trust that He is good, faithful, and loving?

WHAT YOU SAY, DADDY?

Some questions in life do not have easy answers. Share your heart with God on your struggles with the mysteries of your circumstances.

Then simply ask:

"Daddy, will You walk with me through this?"

His answer may not always be an explanation. Sometimes it is His presence, His peace, or a renewed hope in His plans.

No answer does not mean no reason. Some mysteries may be part of our journey of faith. Until then, we can choose to rest in who He is, trust that He is working all things together for good, and believe that His plans are greater than what we can presently see.

PRAYER

Heavenly Father,

There are things in my life that I do not fully understand. Questions that remain unanswered, situations that seem unfair, and pain that still feels difficult to explain.

Help me rest in who You are, even when I cannot understand what You are doing. Remind me that Your goodness, faithfulness, and love do not change simply because I cannot see the full picture.

Teach me to trust that no answer does not mean no reason. Help me accept that some mysteries may be part of my journey of faith, while trusting that You are working all things together for good for those who love and trust You.

When I long for explanations, help me recognize that Your answer for this season may be Your presence, Your peace, or a renewed hope in Your divine plans.

Above all, help me know You more deeply. Teach me to walk by faith, trust Your heart, and rest in the assurance that one day I will see more clearly what I can only glimpse today.

Amen.

CHAPTER 8

I LET GO – TUNG LING BIBLE SCHOOL

"I am leaving."

I remember sitting in front of my boss that day. She sat across the table while I tried to steady my thoughts. I had only been with the company for a little over a year. For the first time in a long while, life had stabilized. I had some savings, I felt comfortable, and Ginny and I did not have children yet. We were enjoying a simple season—short trips, small treats, nothing extravagant, but enough. And yet, I knew I was about to leave all of it behind.

Deep in my heart, there was a clear impression that the Lord was calling me to Tung Ling Bible School. It was not loud or dramatic, but it was firm. Still, sitting there, I struggled. My mind raced with questions. How would she respond? Would she be upset? Would she think I was being irresponsible? I imagined her shouting at me. I had only recently settled into the role, and now I was about to tell her that I was leaving; not for another job or a better opportunity, but because I felt called, with no clear plan for what would come next.

When I finally spoke, I kept it simple. I told her that I felt led to attend Tung Ling Bible School, a six-month full-time course that ran from morning until early afternoon, with coursework and a mission trip at the end. I explained that I could not do it part-time and that I would have to resign. I also told her honestly that I did not know what would come afterwards.

When I finished speaking, I looked up at her. There was a silence that felt much longer than it probably was. She leaned back slightly and thought for a moment. Everything felt suspended. Then she smiled. To my surprise, she said, *"You should go."* She shared that I was still young and did not have children yet. If I did not go now, it would become much harder later. She also told me that she had attended the same Bible school herself, although she had taken the shorter three-month course instead of the six-month leadership program. I was genuinely surprised. I had imagined resistance, perhaps even anger. Instead, the door opened effortlessly. In that moment, I knew God had already gone ahead of me.

As I prepared for Bible school and completed my registration, another challenge emerged. I felt the Lord prompting me to give away all my savings. Not part of it. All of it. I struggled deeply with that impression, but I sensed that the Lord wanted me to learn to depend on His provision. This was the first time I had accumulated enough savings to feel secure.

Ginny and I had just entered a season where we could

enjoy life in simple ways, and now it felt as though everything was being reset to zero. I wrestled with thoughts about how I would survive, knowing that I would be living on small amounts of pocket money from Ginny and functioning almost like a secondary school student again. When I shared this with her, she responded simply: *"The Lord spoke to you. He didn't speak to me."* At the time, it sounded rather direct. Looking back, I realized there was wisdom in it. It would not have been wise for both of us to empty everything. Even without children, we still needed something to live on.

I still remember the first day of Bible school. It was located near my church, and I walked there, knowing it would be easy enough to locate. As I walked along the main road and approached the smaller road leading to the school, a thought suddenly entered my mind; sharp, intrusive, and unsettling. It questioned everything I was doing. *You are being foolish. You have given up a good job. You have given away your savings. You are throwing away certainty for something unknown.*

The thoughts grew louder. *You can still turn back. You can ask for your job again. You can avoid all of this while there is still time.* For a moment, I stopped and walked around the area. It was not merely a passing doubt. It was a genuine struggle—logical, emotional, and spiritual all at once. Eventually, I came to a simple decision. I told God quietly, *"You asked me to do this. So I will go."* And with that, I walked towards the school.

That season at Bible school was deeply impactful. Each morning began with worship, and the presence of the Lord was often tangible. Different speakers and pastors came through, and many of their messages left a lasting impression on me. There was often a simple free lunch in the afternoons. To someone who had given away everything, those meals meant more than they probably should have. I made it a point to be there whenever lunch was available, and it gradually became part of my routine.

One lesson from that season has remained with me to this day. A pastor once spoke openly about one of his greatest regrets. He had spent his life in ministry, constantly helping people and serving others, yet he had neglected the few close friends God had placed in his life. In his later years, he felt profoundly lonely. That lesson stayed with me. It reminded me that while purpose can often be loud, relationships are frequently quiet—and yet they are just as important.

During that season, I was also assigned to assist in the children's ministry for a short period. I remember feeling completely out of place. I was not someone who naturally connected with children, and at that point I did not even have one of my own. Sometimes I would sit alone in the room after everyone had left. The hum of the air-conditioning filled the silence. Everything felt strangely amplified. In those moments, I often found myself asking God why I was there.

At the same time, I spent a lot of time talking with people in ministry, especially men who had already walked that road. They shared honestly about their lives. One pastor told me that whenever he met with youths, he would buy them a drink but not one for himself because he could only afford one. Others spoke about how little they were paid when they first entered ministry. These were not stories of comfort. They were stories of calling. And it became increasingly clear to me that this was what full-time ministry often looked like.

Throughout the entire six months, one struggle remained. I sensed that God might be calling me into full-time ministry, but I could not bring myself to say yes. It was not because I did not love Him. It was because I could not reconcile that calling with my responsibilities. I thought about my parents and the struggles they had endured throughout their lives. I wanted to support them. I thought about my future responsibilities as a husband and father. Even then, I already carried an impression that I would one day have five children. These were real and practical concerns. And I found myself unable to move past them. At the end of the course, I spoke honestly with the Lord. I told Him that I could not take that step. Even when my leader approached me about it, I could not say yes. That decision stayed with me for many years. Quietly. Unresolved.

I often wondered how my life might have turned out if I had said yes. Part of me felt that I had failed. Years later, during a trip to Mozambique, someone prayed for me. She knew nothing about my story. Yet she spoke directly into that hidden struggle. She said that from the moment I was unable to make that decision, God had already prepared another path for me. Something lifted from me instantly. I realized there was no condemnation from Him. He had never held that moment against me. Like a good Father, when I could not take one path, He simply made another way.

Towards the end of Bible school, we went on a mission trip to a closed nation, with several brothers from the course. I remember wading through floodwaters barefoot day after day. The trip stretched us in every way. Yet our hearts were full as we met incredible people and listened to their stories and testimonies. Often, I felt that I received far more than I gave. There was a richness in that simplicity that is difficult to explain.

It took another six months after Bible school before I

found a new job. In total, the journey lasted about a year. But by then, something inside me had already changed. It was not my circumstances. It was my heart. Sometimes obedience is not about getting everything right. It is simply about taking the step we know we are called to take and trusting that God will meet us there.

REFLECTION

LOOKING BACK

Has there been something valuable in your life that you found difficult to release or surrender?

A DEEPER QUESTION

Could God be inviting you to loosen your grip on something good so that you can receive something even greater from Him?

WHAT YOU SAY, DADDY?

Sometimes God asks us to release something He had placed in our hands.

The next time you find yourself holding tightly to a plan, dream, opportunity, or comfort, talk honestly with Him.

Tell Him what you are afraid of losing.

Then simply ask:

"Daddy, what are You inviting me to receive by letting go?"

His ways are often higher than ours. What feels like a loss today may become the doorway to a deeper relationship, greater purpose, and new encounters with Him.

PRAYER

Heavenly Father,

Thank You that Your plans are always better than anything I could design for myself, even when I do not immediately understand them.

Help me trust You enough to release what You ask me to surrender. Teach me to hold Your gifts with open hands, knowing that everything I have comes from You and ultimately belongs to You.

Give me courage to release what You are asking me to release and faith to follow where You lead.

Teach me that obedience is not about losing freedom but the key to gaining access to the life You intended for me all along.

Help me walk with open hands and an open heart.

Amen.

CHAPTER 9

HEAVEN DRAWS NEAR: MOZAMBIQUE

"I *went hungry for days until I felt like dying. The bigger boys beat me up over the food I found in the garbage."* He said it without emotion, almost as though it were normal. There was no anger. No tears. Just a simple statement.

I stood there looking at him, trying to process what I had just heard. This was not a story in a book. This was not a testimony shared from a stage. This was a young boy standing right in front of me, telling me what life had been like. He had lived on the streets, searching through rubbish for something to eat. Even then, older boys would beat him and take whatever food he found. Many times, he went hungry. Yet as I listened to him, I realized that this same boy was now one of the most anointed children I had ever encountered.

That was Mozambique. It was a place where suffering and the presence of God existed side by side. It was a place where the things I had read about in the Bible felt alive and real; not distant stories from history, but something taking place every day.

I had signed up for the trip some time earlier. There was already a hunger in me to see signs, wonders, and miracles; not merely to hear about them, but to witness them firsthand.

When the opportunity came through a ministry organization, I committed to going. But by the time the trip arrived, my personal circumstances had changed. I had left my job and was searching for another one. During that season, Ginny and I moved into my mother-in-law's home. We were all sharing a small room. It felt almost like a dormitory, with a small table and barely enough space to move around. We had given away or stored much of our furniture and belongings.

I remember sitting there and wondering what kind of a season this was. One moment, we had our own flat, hosted cell groups, and lived in a home that felt like a testimony of God's provision. The next moment, we were living in a cramped room while I searched for work. Logically, it made no sense to go on the mission trip. It was expensive. We needed the money. We needed stability. Yet deep inside, I kept sensing that the Lord wanted me to go. More than once, I felt that strong impression to go and not worry about the finances. When I spoke to Ginny about it, she agreed. That gave me the peace to move forward, even though I continued to wrestle with the decision while preparing and packing.

We were heading into rural areas; what they called the "bush bush"; places where some people might never have seen a foreigner before. We did not know what conditions we would encounter. There were more than twenty people in the team from different parts of the world, including about five of us from Singapore.

After a long journey, we arrived at the base in Pemba, where we would spend about eight days. From the moment I arrived, I knew I had stepped into a different world. I had been to Uganda before, and that trip had left an impression on me because of a death that I had heard which involved our hotel guard and a troublemaker. The hotel guard had shot him. So to me, Africa had always carried a sense of risk. But Mozambique felt different. It was as though I had stepped into another reality altogether.

At the base, there were meetings, schedules, discussions, and a Harvest School where we spent time with the students. One evening, during a gathering, a speaker began sharing testimonies about the Holy Spirit. Then he said, *"The Holy Spirit is coming."*

I remember sitting there with my Singaporean mindset immediately analyzing what was happening. There were more than a hundred people in the hall, mostly young adults. As he continued saying, *"He's coming. He's coming"*, I wondered whether this was real. Then he slowly swept his arm across the room from left to right, turning his body as he did so, while declaring that the Holy Spirit was moving in that direction. Suddenly, something happened. It was as though an invisible wave swept through the hall.

People did not fall one at a time. It was almost as though

something moved through the crowd in waves, with people being slain in the Spirit in succession, like a wave sweeping across from one side of the room to the other. I was stunned. Part of me was in awe. Another part of me was still trying to process what I was seeing.

I believed in signs, wonders, and miracles, and I had experienced some myself. But this was unlike anything I had seen before. I even remember wondering what it would mean if nothing happened to me. There was still that logical side of me trying to interpret everything. Yet regardless of my internal questions, one thing was undeniable. The power of the Holy Spirit was real.

What struck me even more was that it was not centered on preaching. I had just completed Tung Ling Bible School and was familiar with structured teaching, sermon preparation, and theological training. This felt different. It felt much closer to what I read in the Book of Acts. There were testimonies everywhere; healings, restorations, miracles—and yet nobody seemed particularly impressed by them. To them, it was simply normal life with God.

I also remember listening to Heidi Baker share. It was not a typical teaching session. She spoke from her heart about intimacy with the Lord in a way that felt deeply authentic. It was not merely doctrine. It was relationship. It challenged me because it was rooted in experience rather than knowledge alone.

Even the children were part of that culture. They did not have separate programs. They sat with the adults, prayed with the adults, and experienced the presence of God alongside everyone else. The things I witnessed in those children were unlike anything I had seen before.

One boy, perhaps six or seven years old, was praying for people. Suddenly he began saying, *"I'm on fire. I'm so hot."* He insisted there was a fire on his head. We could see he was genuinely struggling with the sensation. We even poured water on him, but he continued saying he felt intense heat. Eventually we asked him to pray for us. When he did, we felt the presence of God in a very tangible way. It was remarkable.

Another thing that struck me was their attitude towards food. Most days they ate rice and beans. Perhaps once a week there would be chicken. After meals, when only bones remained, some of the children would pray for God to multiply the food. At first, I thought they were joking. Later, I realized they were completely serious. They had seen too much to doubt. To them, miracles were not theories. They were realities.

We also met a Singaporean lady who was attending Harvest School. She shared how she had struggled academically in university to the point that her parents were called to meet the dean. Then one day, while studying in her hostel room, she heard the words: *"The spirit of excellence is upon you."* From that point onward, everything changed. She eventually graduated as the top student in her cohort. Despite her success, she felt called to missions and chose to follow that path.

We also spent time visiting the children's homes. Each home had a "mama" who cared for the children. I remember taking some of them out for a meal. One of the boys ordered a fish but ate only half of it. I repeatedly encouraged him to finish the rest, at first assuming he was simply full. Later, I discovered he was saving the other half to bring back to his mama. That simple act of love deeply moved me.

The same boy who had told me about surviving on the streets was also extraordinarily gifted musically. He could sing beautifully and play instruments with remarkable ability. Heidi Baker had personally brought him in. Even when he ran away multiple times, she kept searching for him and bringing him back. Eventually, he stayed because he realized he was genuinely loved. That love transformed him.

LIFE THERE WAS NOT EASY. A drought had left water in short supply. For several days, we had enough only for drinking and brushing our teeth. We did not shower. We were covered in dust and mud. We slept on bunk beds, used latrines, and dealt with insects and spiders. It was a very different world from the one we were used to.

One moment that stayed with me involved a delivery of clean water. Large tanks were placed near the entrance, and people from outside came to collect what they needed. Someone asked whether the gates should be closed. The response was simple: *"No. Let them have the water. That's why we're here."* Even when resources were limited, they chose generosity. And somehow, there always seemed to be enough.

Another time, we were delayed before heading into the rural areas. Later, I discovered that they were trying to raise money for fuel. They literally had to pray for fuel. That reality humbled me deeply.

Throughout the trip, there were many moments that

impacted me. One of them was seeing a businessman who had brought his young children with him. He had been there before and was so affected by the experience that he wanted his children to encounter it for themselves. That planted a seed in my heart. One day, I wanted to bring my own children there so they could experience God in a real and tangible way.

When we eventually flew to South Africa on our way back to Singapore from Mozambique, the contrast was overwhelming. We checked into a hotel. There was a buffet. Everything felt abundant.

As I ate, I felt strangely uncomfortable. Only a short distance away, people were living with so little. Yet here there was more than enough. Later, while taking a shower, I spoke to God. I told Him that I had never experienced anything like Mozambique. I told Him that what I had seen there was real. Then I made a promise. I mentioned an amount of money that I did not have, and had never possessed. I told Him to bless me with that amount so that I could give it to the ministry. That became something deeply personal between God and me. And I have never forgotten it.

Mozambique changed me. I had seen miracles before, but not at that level. I had never seen children so familiar with the presence of God, so comfortable experiencing Him as part of daily life. It made me reflect on what truly matters. Children can have comfort, entertainment, opportunities, and every advantage we can provide. But what matters most is that they know God: not merely through information, but through experience.

That trip left me with one clear conviction. Love is not

merely something we say. Love has a face. Love is lived out. Love is demonstrated, especially towards the least of these. If it can happen there, it can happen anywhere. But it requires us to lean on the Lord rather than our own strength, intellect, or resources, and to walk with Him in that reality.

REFLECTION

LOOKING BACK

Have you ever encountered a person, place, or situation that challenged your understanding of God and left you wanting to know Him more deeply?

A DEEPER QUESTION

Is there a part of your heart that longs for more than simply knowing about God—to experience His tangible presence and power, and walk with Him more intimately?

WHAT YOU SAY, DADDY?

There is always more of God than what I know, more than what I have experienced, and more than what I can imagine. Tell Him your heart's desire to stay hungry for more of Him.

Then simply ask:

"Daddy, show me more of who You are."

Miracles, provision, and breakthroughs are wonderful gifts, but they are only a glimpse of who He is. The deeper invitation is not simply to experience what He can do, but to know Him more deeply. There is always more of Him to discover.

PRAYER

Heavenly Father,

Thank You that You are the same God today as You were in the pages of Scripture. You still speak, heal, provide, guide, and reveal Yourself to those who seek You.

Forgive me for the times I have become over-familiar, or easily satisfied with knowing about You while missing opportunities to know You more deeply.

Create within me a greater hunger for Your presence. Help me not to settle for second-hand stories when You invite me into my own journey with You.

Open my eyes to recognize Your hand at work in both the ordinary and extraordinary moments of life. Draw me closer to Your heart and reveal Yourself in fresh ways.

More than miracles, more than blessings, and more than answers, help me desire You above all else.

Amen.

CHAPTER 10

THE GOD WHO STILL HEALS TODAY

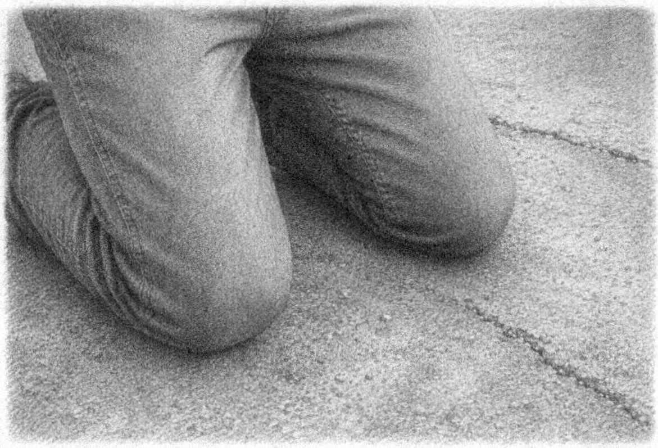

"Can I pray for you?" I did not always have an interpreter, so I did my best to communicate with the long queue of villagers. Some smiled. Some declined. But most were open to prayer.

I remember arriving at the village early in the morning and seeing a queue that stretched further than I could see. Villagers had come from afar—many had travelled long distances. Some were weak. Some were limping. Others were simply holding on to hope that something might change that day. That was the rhythm of our days during the Honduras mission trip.

The doctors attended to their medical needs, while we moved down the queue praying for each person. Every so often, we would hear clapping and cheering break out from different parts of the line. That usually meant someone had just been healed. The rhythm continued throughout the day. Pray. Ask whether anything had changed. Then celebrate as another person testified of healing. We were there in love, witnessing firsthand the love and power of God touching lives. What I did not expect was this: In the midst of praying for others, God would choose to heal me.

The first time it happened was during that Honduras trip. The trip itself had not been an easy decision. Ginny was pregnant with James, our first child, and it was still early in the pregnancy. Naturally, many people advised against her going. The journey would be long; more than twenty hours with transit—and the mountain conditions would not be easy. But Ginny prayed. And in that quiet place, she felt the Lord assure her that He would protect her and everything within her. That was enough for her. So we went.

At the same time, I was dealing with piles, something I had not really shared with others. I had been bleeding badly. It had troubled me for years, but just before the trip, it became particularly severe. I remember wondering whether I should cancel the trip and undergo surgery instead. Yet deep inside, there was a quiet conviction: Entrust it to the Lord. So I went.

The journey was not easy. The flights were long. The bus rides through the mountains were rough. Ginny felt unwell through much of it. Every part of the trip stretched us physically. But once we arrived, something shifted. We stepped into what we had come to do. It was a medical mission trip, and my role was simple: Pray. So day after day, that was what I did.

We were tired, jet-lagged, and constantly traveling between villages. Yet there was something about serving, giving, and standing in the presence of God that carried us through. Then, around the third day, I realized something. I had stopped bleeding. There was no dramatic moment. No one had prayed for me. In fact, no one even knew about my condition. I had been so occupied praying for others that I had not noticed what was happening. But when I checked, it was obvious. No pain. No bleeding. It was gone.

I stood there quietly, trying to make sense of it. There was no single moment I could point to. It had simply happened. And in that moment, I understood something I had never fully grasped before. Sometimes, in the very act of pouring ourselves out to minister to others, God heals us, too.

That trip was filled with moments like that; moments of healing, restoration, and lives being touched. Every day brought testimonies. Twenty. Thirty. Sometimes even fifty reports of healing. It felt as though the Lord was walking with the team every step of the way. But one moment stood out differently.

I was speaking to an elderly man through an interpreter. I explained that we were there to help him, pray for him, and serve his community. He asked where I was from. *"Singapore,"* I replied. He did not know where that was, so I tried to explain. Slowly, he began to understand just how far we had travelled. Then his expression changed. His eyes filled with tears. *"You came all the way here... just to help us?"* There was a pause. Then he began to cry. Not loudly. Not dramatically. Just quietly and deeply. Something shifted in him that day. It was not about what we said. It was about what he saw. Love had become real to him. And through that encounter, he gave his life to Jesus.

THE SECOND HEALING came very differently. I was standing in the overflow room during a healing meeting. People were lining up for prayer while the speaker ministered in the main hall. There was a sense of expectation in the room, as though something more than what we could see was taking place. I stepped forward and began to pray. As I waited on the Lord, I found myself thinking about my right knee. It had been troubling me for years. During my national service days, I had worn down my kneecap. Since then, squatting and kneeling had often been painful.

As I stood there, something unusual began to happen. I felt heat around my kneecap. Not just warmth, but a deep, concentrated heat. It felt almost alive, as though something was moving around the joint. I shifted slightly, trying to understand what I was feeling. No one had touched me. No one had prayed for me directly. Yet the sensation continued. After a while, I tested it. I bent my knee. Then I squatted. No pain. I stood up and tried again. Still no pain. I was healed. In that moment, I realized something simple. When God chooses to act, He does not need a healing process.

THE THIRD HEALING came in a much gradual way. By then, I was in my forties, and my left knee had begun to wear out as well. The pain made it difficult to kneel. That affected me more than I expected because kneeling before the Lord meant a great deal to me. I remembered something my senior pastor once said. He prayed that he would always be able to kneel before God. I found myself praying the same prayer. *"Lord, I want to kneel before You."*

Around that time, Ginny and I felt led to attend a conference in Amsterdam. It was not particularly convenient, but we sensed that we should go. During one of the sessions, there was a call for healing. This time, Ginny prayed for me. She prayed once. Nothing obvious happened. She prayed again. It felt slightly better. She prayed a third time. There was some improvement, but no dramatic breakthrough. And that was it. The meeting ended. We returned to Singapore. Life continued as normal. Then, sometime later, I realized something. The pain was completely gone. I could kneel without discomfort. There was no single moment I could point to. No specific day I could identify. It had simply healed. Quietly. Completely.

Looking back at all three healings, I began to notice something. Each one was different. One happened while I was praying for others. One happened instantly. One unfolded gradually over time. And through that, I learned something deeper. God is not limited to one method. He is not bound by our expectations. He heals as He chooses; personally, intentionally, and often in ways we do not anticipate.

Even now, whenever I pray for someone, there is a quiet prayer that rises within me: *"Lord, as You have healed me, heal them also."* Because I know He can. I have seen Him do it. And every time He does, I am reminded once again: He is near. He is present. And He is still healing today.

REFLECTION

LOOKING BACK

Have you ever prayed earnestly for healing, breakthrough, or a miracle and wondered why the answer seemed delayed or never came at all?

A DEEPER QUESTION

If healing ultimately belongs to God, can you trust Him even when His timing, method, or answer differs from your expectations?

WHAT YOU SAY, DADDY?

God still heals today. Yet many of us carry questions when healing does not come as quickly or as completely as we hope for.

Tell Him honestly about your hopes, disappointments, and fears. Then simply ask:

"Daddy, what are You saying to me as I wait for my healing?"

Healing belongs to Him. Our part is to trust, believe, pray, and persevere while keeping our hearts close to His—gaining strength, peace, or a deeper revelation of who He is.

PRAYER

Heavenly Father,

Thank You that You are still our Healer today.

Help me not to lose heart when healing seems delayed or when answers do not come as quickly as I hope. Strengthen my faith to keep believing, keep praying, and keep trusting You.

Teach me to persevere—not only for myself, but also for those I love and stand in prayer for. Help me align my heart with who You are rather than what I currently see.

Remind me that delays do not always mean denial. Sometimes healing comes instantly. Sometimes it unfolds over time. Yet through every season, You remain faithful.

Help me to keep asking, keep seeking, and keep knocking. Fill me with hope, courage, and expectancy as I place every need into Your hands.

Above all, help me know You more deeply and trust that You are always good, always loving, and always worthy of my faith.

Amen.

CHAPTER 11

HE LOVED CAMBODIA FIRST

"*Look at the women. Redeem this for Me.*" The words came suddenly and pierced deeply into my spirit as I stood facing a low building in a red-light district in Cambodia.

I stood silently, watching the women beneath the neon lights. Some forced smiles towards passing strangers. Others sat quietly in corners, casting quick glances at those who walked by. Loud music echoed through the streets while men called out to passersby. Everything appeared vibrant on the surface. Yet beneath it all was a heaviness that was impossible to ignore.

As I walked through the narrow streets, I did not sense God's judgment. I felt His ache. His compassion. His grief. I sensed the Father's heart towards the women standing there. Many carried stories no one could see from the outside;

stories of brokenness, abuse, abandonment, poverty, survival, and hopelessness. They seemed like strangers in their own land. I could feel the Lord's love for them. And my own heart ached. Yet alongside that burden was a feeble sense of helplessness.

Standing beside me that night were a missionary leader and a missionary lady. Together, we quietly observed the streets before us. There were moments of silence as each of us pondered what we were seeing. Eventually, I shared what I sensed in my spirit. We spoke with hope, knowing that the Lord desired to reach these women. Then I said: *"May God give us a place here."*

Before leaving, we took a simple selfie together. At that time, it seemed insignificant—just three ordinary people standing in the middle of a broken place. Looking back now, I realize it became a pivotal moment in my Cambodia journey.

The interesting thing was that Cambodia had already been growing quietly within my heart long before that night. The Lord had been sharing His heart for the nation. During a significant conference, there was a moment during the final prayer session when people were praying for different nations. As I prayed, I sensed the Lord asking me very clearly: *"Do you want Cambodia?"*

The question carried tremendous weight. It felt far deeper than simply liking a nation or being interested in missions. It felt as though the Lord was asking whether I was willing to carry His burden for the people there. My response came immediately. *"Yes, Lord. I want Cambodia."*

At that same moment, I sensed that one day I would need to spend extended time there; not merely on short mission trips, but living among the people, understanding the land,

and investing into it. Later during that same prayer session, I also sensed Vietnam strongly alongside Cambodia. Deep within me, I heard these words: *"Cambodia and Vietnam shall be saved."*

THE CAMBODIA JOURNEY began during a church service as I was speaking to the Lord about what He wanted me to do. I simply sensed Him say: *"Go to Cambodia."* That was it. No further instructions. No explanation. No timeline. Just go.

At that time, Cambodia was not even a country I thought much about. I knew where it was geographically, but I had no real understanding of the nation, its culture, or why God would suddenly place it on my heart. I wrestled with it for a while, but I knew one thing clearly: I needed to go first before the Lord would reveal more.

The only connection I had there was through one of my former bosses. He had left his corporate role and moved to Cambodia for a season to support family members involved in missionary work. So I contacted him and simply shared that I felt led to come. His response was immediate. *"Just come and stay with us."*

I still remember flying there without any real agenda. I stayed with him and his family while observing the work they had there. People would ask me why I had come to Cambodia, and honestly, I did not know how to answer beyond saying that I felt the Lord had asked me to come. That first trip was mostly about understanding. It was about seeing the people, experiencing the land, and simply soaking in Cambodia.

I walked through the streets, listened to people's stories, visited local shops, and quietly observed daily life. On the surface, it seemed uneventful. Yet something had already begun forming quietly within me. Over the following years, Cambodia kept returning to me again and again. I would make trips there even without a clear agenda. Sometimes they did not appear to be ministry trips at all. I would simply fly in, reconnect with the few people I knew, walk around the city, and seek the Lord concerning His will.

There were moments when I genuinely wondered whether I was meant to relocate there for a season. At one point, I even brought my parents to Cambodia while trying to make sense of what God was doing. I explored possible accommodations, thought through practical arrangements, and continued asking the Lord what exactly He wanted me to do there. Then one day, I sensed the Lord impress something unusual upon my heart: *"Hotels for missionaries."* The phrase stayed with me.

At the time, Airbnb was not yet widely known, so I did not fully understand what it meant. As the months passed, the journey became draining. A friend commented that hotels required millions of dollars to own and operate. I remember feeling discouraged. Yet I also knew that I needed to hold on to what the Lord had spoken. Surely, He had a plan.

One night, I had a vivid dream in which a church leader spoke to me about Cambodia. In the dream, he asked what I had done since the previous season. There was a strong sense that many things had been started but had not yet been fully pursued. I remember bringing up financial limitations. Yet my explanation was almost ignored. The emphasis was not on the obstacles. The emphasis was on continuing to press forward. When I woke up, the dream lingered heavily in my spirit. It felt like a reminder from the Lord not to give up on Cambodia.

Around that same period, I began hosting missionaries who visited Singapore. Through those relationships, I got to know people who had been serving long-term in Cambodia. Then, through my pastor, I was introduced to a couple from church who were involved in hospitality businesses and Airbnb operations in different countries. My pastor simply felt that we should meet. So we did. At first, it was just conversation. We shared stories, experiences, and burdens. But the more we talked, the more I sensed alignment. They viewed hospitality not merely as a business, but as ministry; a way of creating beautiful spaces where people could rest, heal, gather, and encounter God's love through genuine care and presence.

Around that same time, another important connection took place. I had originally arranged to meet a missionary leader in Cambodia. At the last minute, however, he felt strongly led to bring along a lady from his team—a long-term missionary who had faithfully served there for many years. That meeting changed everything. The moment we started talking, it felt like a divine appointment. We were complete strangers, yet it seemed as though God had been preparing each of us separately long before we ever met.

As we shared about Cambodia, missions, hospitality, and the people we felt burdened for, we slowly realized that many of the things God had spoken to each of us individually connected together remarkably well. Everything flowed naturally. Before long, we knew we should do something together, even if it began simply with gathering to pray.

Interestingly, this missionary lady was also an award-winning barista from Canada. Long before any café idea emerged, God had already led her through seasons of learning café operations and artisan coffee preparation. Initially, she did not fully understand why. She simply believed that one day God would use those skills and experience. Only later did it begin to make sense.

Eventually, the three parties came together; the hospitality couple, the missionary lady, and me. We sat together and shared our hearts, our burdens, and the things we believed God had been speaking over the years. The more we talked, the more everything aligned. As we prayed, I received a vision. I saw the three of us clothed in royal robes and wearing crowns. Then we opened our hands before the Lord, and into our hands came gems, resources, manpower, and everything needed for the work ahead. I even saw workers being released to support the assignment.

The impression was simple: If God had truly called us, He Himself would provide what was necessary. It genuinely felt orchestrated by Him. There was a strong sense that this was not merely about business. Not merely about accommodation. Not merely about coffee. It was about creating a place of light for people to gather. A place where conversations could happen naturally. A place where the local community could gather. A place where dignity, kindness, and hospitality could quietly reveal the love of God. A place where local people could receive training, find meaningful employment, and support their families.

Eventually, we found a double-story building. The upper floor became Airbnb accommodation. The ground floor became a café. Step by step, everything began coming together. Even the café equipment arrived in an unexpected way. Around that same time, another ministry-related café in Cambodia had closed down. Much of its equipment and furnishings became available, and we were able to acquire many of the items we needed at a reasonable cost.

Looking back, it truly felt as though God had been arranging the pieces long before we arrived. Renovations began. Licenses were processed. Operations slowly took shape. And eventually, the Airbnb and café opened.

The atmosphere of the place felt special from the very beginning. It was not large or extravagant, yet there was a warmth within it. The coffee was genuinely excellent. Even today, I still remember thinking it was the best coffee I had ever tasted. I am not even an artisan coffee drinker, yet there was something distinct about it. But more than the coffee, I remember the people. The conversations. Their stories. The relationships. The sense of purpose.

Local people were trained in artisan coffee-making and hospitality skills. Relationships formed naturally within the community. Conversations happened organically over meals and coffee. It felt less like operating a business and more like creating a space where light could quietly exist in the midst of brokenness.

I remember one elderly woman who came into the café but could not afford a drink. So they blessed her with a free cup of coffee. She sat there enjoying both the coffee and the atmosphere that the staff helped create. The joy in her eyes deeply touched the team. It was such a blessing to be a blessing.

Ginny and I made many trips back and forth during that season. On one occasion, we even brought James along when he was less than a year old. The missionaries graciously helped care for him so that Ginny and I could spend some time together. Slowly, Cambodia became woven into our family story.

AROUND THAT SAME PERIOD, there were many visions and impressions that deepened what God was placing in my heart. One night, I had a vivid vision of a young Asian woman who had been kidnapped. Her hands, feet, and mouth were tightly bound as she lay helpless in a truck alongside many other women and children. Later, I saw them being taken into brothels and places of captivity. What struck me most was not merely the physical bondage. It was the hopelessness. The loss of dignity. The sense that freedom no longer seemed possible.

In the vision, one of the women eventually stopped resisting altogether. She simply resigned herself to her condition and continued surviving day after day. I remember praying intensely that those held captive would be set free.

On another occasion, someone shared a vision they had received while praying for me before one of my Cambodia trips. They saw the Lord handing me a ladder as I stepped into a foggy land. The image reminded them of Caleb and Joshua entering the Promised Land while others saw only fear and impossibility. That word stayed with me because Cambodia often felt exactly like that. Foggy. Unclear. Without a roadmap. Yet somehow, God kept asking me to move forward one step at a time.

Around that same season, Ginny and I planned another

trip to Cambodia. As I prayed, I kept wondering what exactly the Lord wanted us to do there. One location repeatedly came to mind—the building in the red-light district. I often wondered what it might eventually become. Sometimes I imagined that, if the resources ever came, the old structure could be rebuilt into something larger overlooking the Mekong River.

There was another vision during a worship session that marked me deeply. I saw a Cambodian girl around seven or eight years old. Her hair was rough and windblown. Her clothes were torn and dirty. There was a weariness in her eyes far beyond her years. Suddenly, she fell to the ground. As she collapsed, she became a frail young woman crawling weakly towards me. She could barely move before falling face down once again. In the vision, I felt uncertain and overwhelmed. I was simply a young man, dressed almost like an ordinary tourist. Yet instinctively, I knelt down and held her hand. The moment I touched her, life began returning to her body. Strength returned to her frail frame. She appeared physically restored. Yet even then, she had not fully awakened. She remained in a state of partial consciousness.

That vision stayed with me because I sensed the Lord was showing me something beyond physical poverty. He was revealing woundedness, hopelessness, and captivity of the soul.

Later, I felt strongly led to fast and pray specifically for Cambodia. During that season of prayer, I saw another vision. Two young girls were trapped inside a cage while an enemy prepared weapons against them. Yet one side of the cage was already open. They could have escaped physically. But they were too traumatized and broken within themselves to move.

Again, I felt the Lord's heart for redemption. Not merely freedom from external oppression. But healing from the wounds that kept people imprisoned internally. During that same fast, I repeatedly sensed the month of April. Later, I discovered that 17 April 1975 was the date the Khmer Rouge captured Phnom Penh and began the devastating rule of Pol Pot, resulting in the deaths of millions.

During that season of prayer, I also saw a translucent pearl-white garment descending towards me. It carried different shades of color within it, and somehow, I knew I was meant to wear it.

Around that period, several people independently prayed for me and shared words concerning Cambodia. One person shared Jeremiah 33:3 (NKJV): *"Call to Me and I will answer you, and show you great and mighty things, which you do not know."*

Another person described a vision of vast green harvest fields already prepared. They saw me wearing a straw harvesting hat and walking into those fields, ready to reap the harvest. Again and again, they repeated the same words: *"Do not forget Cambodia."* They believed the harvest was already ready. That Cambodia remained part of God's call on my life.

Another person shared that what God was showing me concerning Cambodia was not about directly fighting darkness, but about bringing His light into dark places and allowing Him to do the battling. That resonated deeply with me. Because throughout the entire Cambodia journey, the focus was never merely darkness. It was always redemption.

EVENTUALLY, COVID struck, and the café and Airbnb could no longer continue because of financial pressures. The closure was painful and confusing. When something feels so clearly orchestrated by God, it is natural to assume it will continue for many years. Perhaps it will expand. Multiply into other locations. Grow into something much larger. What many would consider success. Yet when I asked the Lord about the closure, I sensed Him say something very simple: *"It is finished."*

Not failed. Finished. There was a deep sense of peace in the way He spoke. I sensed that whatever He had intended to accomplish during that season had already been accomplished, even if we could not fully see or understand it. Yet at the same time, He reminded me not to forget Cambodia. I knew there was still more to come. But I also sensed that a new season was beginning for me in another land—Nagaland.

When I look back now at the entire journey—the visions, the prayers, the burden for the women, the café, and the repeated reminders not to forget Cambodia—I realize something important. This story was never initiated by me. It began with Him. Because long before I ever loved Cambodia, He already did.

REFLECTION

LOOKING BACK

Have you ever encountered a person, place, or situation that seemed too broken to ever be restored?

A DEEPER QUESTION

What have you concluded as beyond hope, restoration, or redemption—but God has not?

WHAT YOU SAY, DADDY?

The next time you encounter a person, place, or situation that seems beyond hope, pause for a moment.

Tell God honestly what you see.

Then simply ask:

"Daddy, what do You see that I cannot see?"

What appears impossible to us is often not impossible to Him. Where we see brokenness, He may see redemption. Where we see failure, He may see destiny.

Nothing is too broken, too lost, or too far gone for God.

PRAYER

Heavenly Father,

Thank You that You see value where others see failure, beauty where others see brokenness, and possibility where others see hopelessness.

Help me become more like You. Remove pride, prejudice, and indifference from my heart.

Teach me to love people not because they deserve it, but because You first loved me.

May my life reflect Your compassion and kindness wherever I go.

Amen.

CHAPTER 12

TEN SECONDS OF COURAGE – PAPA FOUNDATION

The toilet smelled. Not just bad, but deeply soaked-in—the kind of smell that comes from years of dog urine and never quite leaves, no matter how much cleaning is done. I stood there trying not to breathe too deeply, holding my breath for as long as I could.

That season of my life felt exactly like that toilet. I was around thirty or thirty-one years old, in between jobs and financially stretched. We had recently welcomed our first son, James, and to remain financially secure, we had rented out our own home and moved in with my mother-in-law. My wife, my son, and I squeezed into a small space together.

Every day, I used that same kitchen toilet—the one the family dog had used for years. The dog was never properly trained and relieved itself wherever it wanted. It was not merely uncomfortable. At times, it felt miserable.

One night, in the middle of that season, I remembered something my senior pastor had said during a sermon: *"Ten seconds of courage. Dream with the Lord."* Just ten seconds. I wrestled with the idea. *Will this even work?* Eventually, I decided to try. Right there, in that toilet, I focused my attention on the Lord. I had no idea what I was going to say. I did not know what would happen. So what came out surprised even me. *"God, give me a skyscraper. And from the rental income, we will support ten thousand children around the world in their education."*

I had not planned that thought. It simply came. And somehow, it made sense in my heart. *"Alright, Lord. We're done."* I almost felt relieved. Then I opened the door. As I stepped out, I sensed the Lord speak in a way that was plain and unmistakable. Not loud. Not dramatic. Just clear. *"Go. Start a foundation."* I paused. Start a foundation? With what?

At that point, I did not even have my own home to live in. There were no further instructions. No roadmap. No explanation. Just a simple statement that made very little sense to me at the time. I did not act on it immediately because I had no idea what to do with it.

Life continued. Days became months. Months became years. Responsibilities increased. Circumstances changed. Many things came and went. But that instruction never left me. *"Go. Start a foundation."* It remained quietly in the background, never demanding attention, yet never disappearing.

Years later, during the COVID season, everything slowed down. In that stillness, the instruction surfaced once again. As

I reflected on the promises, visions, and impressions God had given over the years, I found myself asking: *"Lord, how?"*

I had no strategy. I did not even know where to begin. As I sat with that question, a face came to mind; someone I had met years earlier during a mission trip in Bangalore. We had not spoken for a long time. Yet the impression was strong enough that I reached out. And through *Facebook*, we reconnected. What seemed like a simple conversation became a doorway I never expected. At that stage, I did not mention the foundation. I simply kept the impression in my heart, sensing that she might somehow become part of what God was doing.

Not long afterwards, during a church service, another prompting came. *"Go to Nagaland."* I had never been there. In fact, I often joked that I knew about Disneyland but had never heard of Nagaland. But by then, I had learned something. When God says go, clarity rarely comes first. Obedience does. So I went.

That was where I met Senti and her husband, JJ. We spent time talking, praying, and simply being present together. They showed me around, and in many ways, it felt like a preparation trip—almost like spying out the land. Nothing outwardly dramatic happened. Yet something inside me settled. It felt like standing at the edge of something that had not fully formed yet, but was undeniably real.

While on my flight home after my first trip, I asked the Lord what name the foundation should bear. The answer came simply. *"Papa."* As the name came to me, I also saw a vision of the word "Papa." Honestly, it was not a name I would have chosen. It did not sound particularly strategic or impressive. Part of me wondered whether a more sophisticated name might help people notice it. But the more I reflected on it, the more it made sense.

Across many cultures, *"Papa"* means father. And this foundation was never about us trying to help children through our own efforts. It was about the Father's heart reaching for them, caring for them, and providing for them in ways we never could. So as I had learned to do, I followed His choice rather than mine.

After I returned home, things began aligning in ways I could not have orchestrated. Senti was at a transition point in her own journey and was exploring what the next season of her life might look like. There was a shared sense of direction, even though none of us had all the answers. Step by step, we moved forward. It was not fast. It was not perfect. But it was enough to keep going.

From the moment I first sensed the words, *"Start a foundation,"* to the day Papa Foundation was launched, eleven years had passed.

Eleven years. Sometimes I think about that. How easy I could have forgotten about it. How many reasons there were to let it go. How many practical arguments existed against it. And yet the word remained.

The early days were not easy. We did not have the licenses required to raise funds globally, so everything had to begin locally. Resources were limited. There were many uncertainties about long-term sustainability. We deliberately chose not to support more children than we could realistically sustain. We did not want to help for a year or two and then disappear. We wanted to walk with them throughout their educational journey, just as a father would.

Some of the stories were heartbreaking. There were children living in homes affected by drug addiction, where hunger and the absence of education were daily realities. One child had lost his father at a young age. His mother later attempted to take her own life by setting herself on fire with kerosene. Although she survived, she suffered severe burns. The child's guardian became his grandmother, who was over eighty years old and living in a mud house.

Again and again, we witnessed difficult circumstances. Yet God continued providing. He sustained the foundation and enabled these children to remain in school. That alone felt like a miracle.

God also provided practical strategies. Many of the fundraising ideas came through Senti. One particularly significant initiative involved recurring contributions at a small and accessible level so that almost anyone could participate. Within a day, more than a hundred people signed up.

One message especially stayed with me. A person wrote to say that they did not have much money, but they had always wanted to help someone. Now, for the first time, they felt they could. That touched me deeply. It was never about the size of the contribution. It was about giving people an opportunity to participate in something greater than themselves.

Today, Papa Foundation continues to grow. There are new impressions about land, schools, and reaching other nations. Even places like Ukraine have come onto our hearts. But we are not rushing ahead. We are simply taking the next step. Just as it began. There are still unknowns. Still questions. Still moments when we do not have complete clarity. Perhaps that is how it was always meant to be. But one thing remains certain. Heavenly Papa will provide. He cares for the little ones.

As I look back now, I realize that Papa Foundation did not begin with a strategy, a business plan, or a brilliant idea. It began with ten seconds. Ten seconds in a place I would never have chosen. Ten seconds during a season when very little in my life felt promising. Yet that was where the beginning was.

Sometimes the most important moments in our lives are not the ones that appear significant. They often feel small. Quiet. Hidden. Moments when we choose, even briefly, to turn towards the Lord instead of remaining where we are. Moments when we dare to believe beyond what we can currently see.

If there is one thing I have learned, it is this: Do not wait for the perfect conditions. Do not wait for your life to make sense before responding to God. Give Him a moment. Ten seconds, if that is all you have. Be honest with Him. You may not receive the full picture. You may not understand where it will lead. But you might receive something small; a seed, an impression, a simple instruction—that stays with you long enough to change everything that follows.

So take ten seconds. And dream with the Lord.

REFLECTION

LOOKING BACK

Is there a dream, calling, or promise that you have quietly stopped believing for, because it feels impossible?

A DEEPER QUESTION

What might happen if you stopped measuring possibilities by the size of your faith and started measuring them by the size of your God?

WHAT YOU SAY, DADDY?

God often invites us to dream beyond our own abilities.

The next time you think about a dream, burden, or calling on your heart, bring it before Him. Then simply say:

"Daddy, this is my dream that I want to share with You."

His plans are often bigger than our imagination and greater than our resources. Yet He does not ask us for perfect faith. He simply asks us to trust Him with what we have.

A mustard seed of faith in a limitless God is enough.

Keep dreaming. Keep believing. Keep walking with Him.

What God promises, He is faithful to fulfill.

PRAYER

Heavenly Father,

Thank You for the dreams, callings, and desires that You place within my heart.

Give me the courage to dream with You and not limit what You can do because of my own fears, weaknesses, or circumstances. Help me remember that You do not ask for great faith—only faith the size of a mustard seed, placed in a great God.

When the journey feels long and the waiting difficult, help me not to lose heart. Strengthen me to keep believing, keep trusting, and keep walking with You, even when I cannot yet see how Your promises will come to pass.

Teach me to partner with You in faith, knowing that what You initiate, You are able to fulfill. Help me trust Your timing, Your ways, and Your faithfulness.

Above all, draw me closer to You. May my dreams become aligned with Your heart, and may my life become a testimony of what You can do through someone who simply says yes.

Amen.

CHAPTER 13

POSSESSING THE LAND

I walked slowly towards my car, carrying the weight of everything that had been building over the previous weeks and months. When I opened the door and sat down, something inside me broke—but not in despair. It was relief. A deep sense of relief that, humanly speaking, we had done all we could. The rest was now entirely in God's hands. I almost smiled to myself and spoke to the Lord in Mandarin: *"Wah God, You really want to play so big?"*

There is something about speaking to God in Mandarin that feels more intimate and personal to me. In that moment, I recognized a familiar place. It was the place where circumstances had moved beyond human ability. The place where no amount of planning, effort, or calculation could solve what lay ahead. It was now entirely up to Him. Strangely, that did not fill me with the level of anxiety it might have caused others. Because I had already sensed Him say: *"Now it's My turn."* And I knew what that meant. We were covered. He would bring it to pass, just as He had done in every property journey before. With God, nothing is impossible.

When I look back, this was not the first time we had stood in such a place. Our journey with homes had always followed a similar pattern. The first home began simply; with a list and no resources. Just a list of what we hoped for and what we needed. Nothing extravagant. Yet quietly and faithfully, God provided. That home became our starting point, where we first learned that He was not distant, but deeply involved even in the practical details of our lives. The second home was different. It stretched our faith much more.

After selling our first property, we realized we had just enough to move into the next one. Just enough. No buffer. No margin for error. There were competing buyers, competing offers, and several moments when the opportunity could easily have slipped away. But once again, God provided. This time, He did so through a brother in the real estate industry.

The Lord had impressed upon me to look for him when the time came to move. He walked alongside us through the process and helped us navigate the competing offers. In the end, we stepped into that home not because we were especially capable, but because God made a way. Interestingly, his wife is an interior designer who understands our journey of faith and has played a significant role in the renovations of each of our homes. It was in that second home that I began to understand how specific God can be.

I noticed how much space mattered to Hezekiah. There was a time we stayed in a small room in Legoland Malaysia, and he experienced intense meltdowns. It was not simply behavior. There was something deeper at work. Space mattered. The environment mattered. The freedom to move around mattered. Without realizing it then, God had already provided for those needs before Hezekiah was even born.

~

YEARS PASSED, and life settled into a comfortable rhythm. We were happy in Serangoon. The children were growing. My parents-in-law lived with us. Everything was working well. There was no logical reason to move. Yet, quietly and independently, both Ginny and I began sensing the same thing. It was time to move.

The impression did not come dramatically. It did not seem logical. There was no obvious reason to leave a place that had served us so well. But when God calls, the absence of reason does not mean the absence of purpose. So we prayed. We sought confirmation. And over time, the conviction became clear. We were to move.

At the same time, we had to navigate concerns raised by people who loved us. Some questioned our motives and wondered whether we were making the right decision. Honestly, it would have been easier to stay. Much easier.

What lay ahead would become a two-year journey of faith.

Ginny had saw a vision of a map of Singapore highlighting an area in the east that we should consider. It was not highly detailed, but it gave us direction. Around the same period, the Lord also spoke to me about Hezekiah's future school. In a vision, I saw myself moving as though in aerial view, traveling from Parkway Parade towards a particular location. At that time, I did not even know what primary schools were in that area. But I knew this much: Wherever we moved had to align with the school God had prepared for Hezekiah.

I did not fully understand it then. But I knew that God was leading us towards that region. So we took the first step.

Weekends became days of searching. We viewed many homes on our own, learning, observing, and discerning. Over the years, we had come to recognize that when a place is truly where the Lord wants us to be, there is often a particular sense of peace and belonging.

Then we came across one house. It was not impressive. In fact, it was run-down. The condition of the property meant extensive renovations, which would normally have been a no-go for us. There were also many spiritual elements in the house that did not align with our faith. Financially, it would stretch us significantly. Naturally, it was not something we would have chosen. Yet God's ways are often very different from ours. Sometimes He stretches our faith beyond what feels comfortable or reasonable.

As it is written: *"For My thoughts are not your thoughts, Nor are your ways My ways," says the Lord. "For as the heavens are higher than the earth, So are My ways higher than your ways, And My thoughts than your thoughts."* (Isaiah 55:8–9, NKJV)

Over the following months, I had two dreams. In the first, I was walking through a house filled with light. The children were running freely and laughing. There was a deep sense of peace. What stood out most was the rooftop—it was beautiful, and I could see it clearly.

In the second dream, I woke up saying, *"I found it! I found it! I found the house the Lord has for us!"* It was the same house.

That was enough for me. There was, however, a moment that tested my conviction.

One day, as I was walking towards an eatery opposite the property, I had a strong impression of a voice saying, *"This is not the house. You got it wrong."* But something immediately felt off. There was no peace in it. It did not align with what God had already shown me. In that moment, I knew it was not from Him. If anything, it confirmed the opposite. It strengthened my conviction that this was indeed the house, because something seemed intent on pulling me away from it.

Ginny had her own journey through the process. She received impressions and visions as well, though they were less specific than mine. There were moments when she struggled. This house required a significant stretch; financially, emotionally, and practically. There were easier options. Safer options. But obedience rarely feels like the easier path.

Through many conversations, prayers, and repeated visits, we gradually came into alignment; not only with one another, but also with trusted leaders who prayed with us and journeyed alongside us. One particular word from a leader stayed with us. She sensed that this was "the beginning of beginnings" for our family, and that God would use this experience to prepare us for greater things yet to come.

Then came the call. The agent informed us that the owner had a serious buyer and was preparing to close the deal. We had previously asked her to keep us informed because of our interest in the property. Now we had to act. We submitted a bid. It was too low. We kept increasing it. The owner remained firm.

Step by step, the negotiations continued. The property had

been listed and re-listed for years, but this time it was finally moving towards a sale. We knew we had to secure it. This was the house God had shown us. We had not yet sold our existing home. The timing made little sense. Yet we could not shake the conviction that this was where the Lord was leading us.

After a difficult negotiation process, our offer was accepted. As a family, we held hands and did our little family celebration dance. But beneath the joy was a quiet awareness. This was only the beginning. Now we had to sell our second house within a fixed timeline.

That journey stretched us in ways we had never expected. There were nearly two hundred viewings. Weekends were consumed by keeping the house spotless with endless staying out so that potential buyers could view in privacy. We would step out, return home, clean up, and do it all over again. Week after week. It often felt as though we had no place to rest.

During that season, the Lord showed me something significant. I sensed that this new house was like a fortress, supporting the "main castle"; our church, which was located along the same road. There were also visions of spiritual conflict surrounding the place.

In one vision, I saw angels engaged in battle, locked in a stalemate. Then heaven opened, and reinforcements arrived. More angels entered the battle. The impression was clear. This was more than acquiring another property. There was a spiritual significance to the place that we did not yet fully understand. Then the pressure intensified. The deadline drew closer, yet there were still no serious offers. If we could not secure a buyer in time, we would lose our deposit. At any moment, everything could fall apart. Once again, we found ourselves in a familiar place. A place where we had no solution of our own. *"God, it is Your turn."*

Around that time, the same brother in the property industry contacted me. After understanding our situation, he immediately went into solution mode. Even though the deadline had already passed, he kept encouraging me not to give up. He also connected us with the right banker; someone who understood our predicament and proposed a workable, financing solution within minutes.

During that challenging season, God sustained us through people, through prayer, and through quiet reassurance. At that point, only one month remained before we would lose our deposit and, with it, the house the Lord had spoken to us about.

A close couple we knew were also in the process of selling their home. Their testimony was remarkable; they found the right buyer at the right price during their very first viewing. They recommended their agent to us. After assessing our situation, the agent said honestly, *"This will take a miracle."* Then, with only two weeks remaining, the agent called. We had a buyer. A genuine buyer. A good offer. A way forward. We rejoiced as another hurdle was cleared. God had made a way. Yet there were still more steps ahead.

One of them came when we were asked to meet at the law firm and provide the required cheques for the next stage of the purchase; a deposit that we did not yet have. We left the law firm quietly. Neither of us had much to say. Later, we sat together at a nearby restaurant for lunch, eating without really tasting the food. As the head of the household, I felt the weight of it all.

Ginny looked at me, and I knew the question she was asking without either of us speaking. Inside, I was asking God the very same question. *How are we going to pay this deposit?* But this was simply another step in the journey of faith. It was beyond us. It was up to the Lord. And once again, He provided. That milestone was cleared, and then the next. And then the next. Step by step, miracle after miracle, we eventually completed the purchase, moved into the house, and began the renovation process.

One unexpected blessing was that the buyers of our previous home allowed us to remain there until the renovations were completed. That saved us from having to move into temporary accommodation, which would have been especially challenging with elderly family members and young children.

Shortly after we moved in, both of my parents-in-law faced serious situations; one involving a critical medical condition and the other an accident. It was a difficult season. At the time, I was away in Canada on a work trip when these events occurred.

Around that same period, I also sensed that the Lord was leading me to leave my employment. At the same time, our helper had to return to her hometown for several months because her own daughter required surgery. We desperately needed help at home, and Hezekiah was temporarily unable to attend school because of logistical challenges. Everything seemed to converge at once.

When I tendered my resignation, I was unexpectedly granted three months of garden leave. That in itself felt like a miracle, especially since I was not leaving for another job. The timing could not have been better. It allowed me to support my family, assist with the renovations, and be present during a season when we genuinely needed help. It also became a precious period of rest, reflection, and restoration. Looking back, I can see how carefully God had arranged it all. That season eventually ended with a new job offer; one that continued to provide for our family. His faithfulness never failed us.

As I reflect on the location of our home, I am amazed by how many details aligned. The house was within one kilometer of Hezekiah's school; a school I did not even realize I had alumni access to because my former primary school had closed. I later discovered that my alumni status had been transferred to this school. As a result, Hezekiah was admitted during the first round of selection. Only afterwards did I realize that God had been arranging these details long before we ever noticed them. Everything our family needed was already there. God had gone before us. The journey was not easy, but His fingerprints were everywhere.

After we moved in, I had a vision of a river flowing into the house and a well at its centre. I sensed the Lord saying, *"Sing to the well."* So we did. We gathered as a cell group, worshipped together, and prayed. His presence was wonderful among us.

When I look back now—from the first home, to the second, and now to this one, I see a familiar pattern. God calls. It rarely makes sense at first. We hesitate. We wrestle. We obey. And He provides. Not everything at once. Just enough for the next step. And then the next. And then the next. Until one day we realize that we were never walking alone. He was leading us all along.

As we reflect on this home and its location, its space, and

the way it serves our family, it is evident that God planned it with remarkable attention to details. He knew what each person in our household would need. He knew who would come through our doors.

The youth cell gathers here from time to time. Other groups meet here as well. He knew how this home would become a blessing, not only to us but also to others. He honors the right desires of the heart. All He asks is that we believe, obey, and follow.

Because truly, with God, nothing is impossible.

REFLECTION

LOOKING BACK

Has God ever invited you to step into something that felt far bigger than your resources, abilities, or understanding?

A DEEPER QUESTION

Are you waiting for enough resources before saying yes to God, while He is waiting for your yes before revealing His provision?

WHAT YOU SAY, DADDY?

Sometimes God invites us into journeys that make little sense through human eyes.

The next time you find yourself facing something bigger than your abilities, resources, or plans, bring it before Him. Then simply ask:

"Daddy, what are You building that I cannot yet see?"

What seems like five loaves and two fishes in our hands can become more than enough in His. He sees the provision, purpose, and people long before we do.

His invitation is not to have all the answers, but to trust Him enough to take the next step.

PRAYER

Heavenly Father,

Thank You that You often call us into things that are bigger than ourselves, not because we are sufficient, but because You are.

Help me trust You when Your invitations seem beyond my resources, abilities, or understanding. Remind me that You are the God who multiplies five loaves and two fishes, and that what is impossible for me is never impossible for You.

Give me the courage to follow where You lead, even when I cannot see the full journey ahead. Like Abraham, help me trust the One who calls more than the destination itself.

When I focus on what I lack, remind me of Your abundance. When I worry about the future, remind me that You already know every need, every provision, and every life You intend to bless when I take that journey with You.

Teach me to walk by faith, knowing that what You initiate, You also sustain and fulfill.

Amen.

CHAPTER 14

ASK FOR WISDOM

I still remember the moment clearly. I was seated quietly, my laptop open, waiting for the page to load. There was no drama in that moment—just a stillness, the kind that comes after a long journey when you know something is about to be revealed.

When the page finally appeared, I stared at the screen for a few seconds, just to be absolutely certain. A perfect GPA. Dean's List.

I closed my eyes, stood up, and instinctively knelt down. *"Thank You, Lord."* There were no long prayers. No elaborate words. Just gratitude. Because deep inside, I knew this was not something I could have achieved on my own. Without Him, I would never have come this far.

When I think back to how it all started, it was never about chasing grades. For many years, there had been a quiet desire in my heart to pursue a master's degree. In my younger days, I had considered it more than once, but the cost was always a limiting factor. So I postponed it, again and again. Yet every time I drove past the Singapore Management University (SMU) campus, something stirred within me. I would glance at the buildings, watch the students walking in and out, and imagine myself there—sitting in a classroom, learning, engaging, and growing. There was always something about learning that I loved.

One day, after hearing how my church leader had completed his master's degree at SMU with excellent results, I began to consider it more seriously. So I prayed and asked the Lord. The impression was simple. It was a green light. It sounded straightforward. But it was not.

At that time, the children were still young. Hezekiah had just been born. Life was already full; work responsibilities, family commitments, and countless demands competing for time and attention. Yet I stepped into that new season, knowing it would stretch me.

There were many late nights spent at the study table with my laptop open and assignments waiting to be completed, while the sounds of family life continued around me. Often, there was a quiet tension within my heart. Should I spend more time with the children? Or should I push through this assignment? I wanted to honor both. I wanted to be present as a father. And I wanted to honor God by doing my best in what I had committed myself to.

So I learned to become efficient. Every pocket of time mattered. Late nights became normal. Sleeping after one in the morning and waking early for work became part of life for more than a year. Through it all, one simple prayer followed me into every class: *"God, give me wisdom."*

Sometimes I whispered it before a lesson began. Sometimes during class discussions when I did not know what to say. Sometimes before assignments that felt beyond my ability. *"God, give me wisdom."* And time after time, He answered.

Accounting was one of the most challenging modules. Many students struggled with it, and I was no exception. Yet somehow, by God's grace, I was able to do well. Not merely pass. Do well.

Looking back, I never set out to achieve a perfect GPA. That was never the goal. I simply wanted to do my best and honor God in the opportunity He had given me. But semester after semester, the results came back stronger than I expected. Each time, I found myself doing the same thing. Pausing. Kneeling. Thanking God.

Towards the end of the program, I realized something surprising. A perfect GPA was actually possible. So I pressed on. Even the final capstone project went well. Our team received an A. And when everything was completed, I found myself back on my knees again.

This was never about ability. It was always about grace. One of the greatest lessons I learned during that season was both simple and profound. If we need wisdom, we should ask for it.

James 1:5 (NKJV) says:

"If any of you lacks wisdom, let him ask of God, who gives to all liberally and without reproach, and it will be given to him."

At one point, I found myself thinking about all the areas of life where people seek guidance. A coach for their career. A coach for their health. A coach for leadership. A coach for personal growth. Then I sensed the Lord gently ask: *"Why not let Me be your coach for everything?"*

The thought stayed with me. The more I reflected on it, the more it made sense. God knows everything. He understands every field, every situation, and every decision far better than any expert or *guru*. So why not ask Him? What to invest in. What to do. What to eat. How to lead. How to grow.

But it also meant something else. It meant I had to seek Him actively. To listen. To pay attention. Because He would guide. But I had to follow.

My time at SMU did more than give me a degree. It shaped something within me. It awakened an entrepreneurial spirit that had always been there, quietly waiting. Through modules on innovation and entrepreneurship, I began sensing that one day I would build something of my own.

This was not the first time such thoughts had surfaced. Over the years, several prophetic words had been spoken over me suggesting that I would not remain in a traditional corporate role forever. I sensed that one day I would build, lead, and steward something of my own. And that resonated deeply. Business had always been part of my environment growing up. In many ways, I had always wanted to be an entrepreneur.

There was another moment that stayed with me. A missionary once stayed at our home. The next morning, he shared a vision he had received. *"Lex,"* he said, *"I see you as a pastor."* I smiled. It was not the first time I had heard something similar. But then he added: *"I see a badge on you. On the front it says CEO. But on the back, it says pastor."* That stayed with me. Because it captured something I had sensed but never fully articulated. Perhaps I was not called to a traditional pastoral role. Perhaps I was called to carry a pastoral heart into other spaces. To lead people not only in work, but in life.

Interestingly, others noticed this, too. One boss once told me that I was "too pastoral" with my team. It was clear from the tone that it was not meant as a compliment. However, I chose to remain true to who I was, because I needed to stay true to who God had made me to be.

Even today, I remain in contact with some of those former team members. What began as professional relationships eventually became genuine friendships built on care and trust.

During that same season, God was blessing the work of our team. We performed exceptionally well and became the number one sales team among our key partners in the industry. It was not something we had orchestrated. It was simply God's program. Not by might. Not by power. But by His Spirit.

~

AFTER SMU, another prompting came. Harvard. It was not something I had planned.

During a study trip to Boston as part of my master's program, I visited the Harvard campus. As I walked towards the gates, I found myself talking to the Lord about Harvard and wondering whether it was even possible. Then I noticed a sign beside the gate bearing the Harvard logo. It simply read: "One Way." The moment struck me.

Later, during a morning walk in Boston, I found myself talking to the Lord about Harvard once again. As I walked, I began questioning my own motives. *Why did I want to go there in the first place?*

I was thinking out loud, trying to answer that question for myself. Just as I began to say, *"I want to go because I am..."* a large eagle suddenly landed on a rooftop directly in front of me. In that moment, I felt as though the Lord was answering my question. The eagle seemed to symbolize who He had called me to be. The message impressed upon my heart was simple: *"Because you are an eagle."*

The moment felt significant. And somehow, deep within, I knew I would return to Harvard one day. I did not know how. I did not know when. But I knew.

As I sought prayer from others, one person shared a strong impression. She sensed an urgency in the timing. Either I should pursue it now or not at all. There was a window of opportunity that should not be missed, even though it was during the COVID season. That resonated deeply with me. I felt I had to move forward.

When the time came, it made little financial sense. We had three children. I had only recently completed my master's degree. The cost was substantial. The only way forward was through a significant education loan with a ten-year repayment period. I struggled with that. I questioned it repeatedly. Why would God want me to take an education loan? It did not fit my understanding of how God usually works. Yet I continued sensing that He wanted me to proceed.

The loan approval came quickly; far more quickly than I expected. Although I carried the weight of that decision, I also held onto a quiet impression from the Lord: The loan would be cleared much sooner than expected. And eventually, it was. After the sale of our house, the loan was fully paid.

Harvard became another season of stretching. Classes often ran from evening until past midnight, sometimes into the early hours of the morning. The next day, work continued as usual. It was exhausting. But it was also transformative. Not only because of what I learned, but because of how it expanded my understanding of people, cultures, leadership, and possibilities. It was more than education. It was preparation.

Looking back now, I can see how everything connected. Had I not gone to SMU, I would never have achieved the results that opened the door to Harvard. Had I not taken that first step of faith, I would never have entered the next season. Through it all, one truth remained constant. God responds to the posture of the heart. Not perfection. Not ability. But a willing heart that seeks Him.

If there is one thing I have learned from this journey, it is this: Ask for wisdom. Ask again. And keep asking. Because He gives generously. And when He leads, even when it stretches you beyond what feels comfortable, He will also provide. In the end, all the glory belongs to Him.

REFLECTION

LOOKING BACK

Have you ever made a decision that seemed right at the time, but later realized there was a wiser way?

A DEEPER QUESTION

How different might your life look today if God's wisdom had guided every major decision you have made—and how different might your future look if it guided the ones still ahead?

WHAT YOU SAY, DADDY?

God cares about more than life's major decisions. He cares about the everyday moments too. The next time you face a decision—big or small—invite Him into it. Then simply ask:

"Daddy, which should I choose?"

Sometimes wisdom begins with the humility to ask.

As we involve Him in the ordinary moments of life, we learn to recognize His voice, trust His perspective, and discover that His wisdom is often far greater than our own.

A child does not need to have all the answers when he knows he can ask his Father.

PRAYER

Heavenly Father,

Thank You that I do not have to navigate life on my own. Thank You that You promise to give wisdom generously to those who ask.

Teach me to walk in humility and not assume that I always know what is best. Help me remember to seek Your wisdom in both the major decisions and the ordinary moments of life.

Give me a heart that is quick to ask, quick to listen, and willing to follow where You lead. When I am uncertain, remind me that I can always come to You. When I lack wisdom, help me ask with confidence, knowing that You delight in guiding Your children.

Draw me into a deeper relationship with You, where seeking Your guidance becomes a natural part of everyday life. Help me trust Your perspective above my own and recognize that Your wisdom is always greater than mine.

May my choices reflect Your wisdom, my life reflects Your goodness, and my journey bring glory to You.

Amen.

CHAPTER 15

COUNT YOUR DAYS

I still remember the moment clearly. I moved gingerly and sat quietly beside his bed. No words. Just a glance. A simple acknowledgement between us. That was enough.

The hospital room carried a heavy atmosphere, thick with emotion and struggle. His spouse sat faithfully by his side, gently tending to his needs, while I remained seated, watching and praying. By then, he had lost so much weight that he was only a shadow of his former self. He could not speak much. Neither could I. Yet in that silence, everything was understood. I focused on praying for him.

The air felt heavy, as though it carried the weight of everything left unsaid. I stayed there for about thirty minutes, pressing in and asking the Lord for his healing. As I prayed, I saw many visions. I held on to the hope of a miracle. I wrestled for his life. Yet what stood before me was real. Cancer was slowly squeezing the life out of his weakened body.

At one point, I felt prompted to place my hand on his arm and pray more intentionally. This should have been the easiest thing to do. I had prayed for many people before. Yet my arm felt like a millstone. Too heavy to lift. I told myself I would do it during the next hospital visit.

Even today, I do not fully understand why I struggled in that moment. Perhaps it was the reality of what I was witnessing. Perhaps it was the emotions I was carrying for someone so dear to me. Perhaps it was the tension between faith and what seemed to be unfolding before my eyes.

He had a young daughter who was only six years old. His parents had passed away not long before. He had already been battling cancer for more than a year. I loved this brother. And yet, in that moment, it was so difficult to reach out. To this day, there remains a quiet wondering and a slight tinge of regret. Because that was the last time I saw him.

Not long afterwards, he passed away. His death left a deep mark on me. He was almost fifty years old—a life filled with testimonies. He was not only the first cell leader who took over the cell group that Ginny and I had started, but also a beloved brother whom I had known for almost twenty years.

When he first joined us, he was cautious and reserved. But over time, he opened up in his own unique way. He had a distinctive sense of humor. Not every joke drew immediate laughter, but over the years, whenever some of us gathered together, we found ourselves recalling his expressions, his actions, and his funny ways. Those memories never failed to bring smiles and laughter. He was also one of the intellectuals among us. He reflected deeply on Scripture, sermons, and cell group discussions. Often, he would approach me one-on-one to share his thoughts and insights.

He read widely, especially on current affairs, and carried a strong sense of righteousness. He was a passionate man who loved truth and was a genuine disciple of Christ. Yet beyond his humor and intellect, what stood out most was his heart.

Through him, I witnessed another expression of love; one that the world rarely talks about and even more rarely, practices. He was quiet and unassuming. He did not draw attention to himself. Yet he left a lasting impact wherever he went. He paid attention in ways many people overlook. He remembered what others shared, especially their struggles, and carried those burdens in his heart. He asked sincere questions. He reflected on people's situations. He prayed for them quietly. And later, he would check in again; not once, but consistently. There was no desire for recognition. No need to be noticed. He simply cared. There was a purity in the way he loved. Almost childlike in its sincerity. It was not complicated. Not strategic. Not driven by expectation. It was steady. Faithful. Real.

Through him, I learned that loving people is not measured by how much we say or how visible our actions are. It is measured by how deeply we carry others in our hearts before God.

I remember praying about who should take over the cell group. I felt the Lord speak clearly that it should be him. And I was glad when he stepped into that role. In time, he met his spouse, got married, and became a father. His greatest loves were his wife, his daughter, and the Lord. He spoke about them openly and sincerely. He was a loving husband. A devoted father. And a man whose faith in God remained unwavering.

I also remember the day I picked him up for a prayer meeting in church. By then, I had learned that he had been unwell for more than a year. I told him honestly that I was upset he had not shared it earlier. In his gentle way, he replied that he did not want to burden anyone. Like many parents who quietly carry their struggles so that others will not worry, he chose to carry his own.

Although I had once been his cell leader, he taught me far more about loving people than I ever taught him. What stayed with me most were three simple things he shared during one of our final conversations. In his usual style—with a touch of humor and cheekiness—he said: *"Don't work so hard. Spend time with your family and loved ones." "Eat healthily. It costs more, but it is worth it. Take care of yourself." "Trust the Lord with all your heart."*

Those words carried even greater weight after he passed away. Time is precious. We often assume we have many years ahead. That there will always be another opportunity to meet. Another opportunity to speak. Another opportunity to encourage, pray, help, or simply be present. But life does not always unfold that way.

Sometimes the moment before us is the moment. Sometimes the person before us is the assignment.

So do not delay what matters. Do not delay knowing Jesus. Do not delay responding to His voice. Do not delay stepping into what He has placed in your heart. Because time, though we often assume we have plenty of it, is short for all of us.

Yet this is not a message of fear. It is an invitation to know the Father.

In every season of life, there are many voices competing for our attention—our fears, our circumstances, the opinions of others, and even our own doubts. But there is one voice that matters above all.

Will you listen to His voice?

He is not distant. He is your Father. As we learn to listen, trust, and follow, step by step, even when the path seems unclear, He faithfully leads us forward.

You may not see the whole journey. But you can take the next step. And often, that is enough.

So pause. Reflect. Where are you now? What is He saying to you?

Do not wait. Not tomorrow. *Today.*

This life is not merely about getting through each day. It is about stepping into all that He has prepared for you.

A life of purpose.

A life with Him.

An abundant life.

REFLECTION

LOOKING BACK

If you knew exactly how many days remained in your life, would you live differently from the way you are living today?

A DEEPER QUESTION

If today were your last day on earth, would you be confident about where you will spend eternity—and have you responded to God's invitation through Jesus Christ?

WHAT YOU SAY, DADDY?

Life moves quickly. The next time you find yourself reflecting on your future, your goals, or your plans, pause for a moment. Then simply ask:

"Daddy, what is the most important thing I need to do?"

Achievements, possessions, and success all have their place. Yet none of them can follow us into eternity.

The most important decision we will ever make is what we choose to do with Jesus and His invitation to eternal life.

Time is a gift, but none of us knows how much of it remains. If God is speaking to your heart today, do not wait for another day to respond.

PRAYER

Heavenly Father,

Thank You for the gift of life and for every single day that You have given me.

Help me see my life from an eternal perspective. Remind me that success, possessions, achievements, and even the things I spend so much time pursuing are temporary, but my soul is eternal.

Thank You that Your heart desires that none should perish. You have loved me long before I knew You. Thank You for pursuing me throughout my life, even in moments when I did not recognize Your hand.

Help me understand that no amount of effort, good works, achievements, or personal merit can earn eternal life. Thank You that Jesus has already done everything necessary through His death and resurrection to make a way for me to know You and spend eternity with You.

If You are speaking to my heart today, give me the courage to respond. Open my eyes to the gift of salvation that has already been prepared for me. Help me receive by faith what You freely offer through Jesus Christ.

Thank You that You desire not only to save individuals, but entire families, generations, and those we love. May Your love, grace, and truth draw many to You.

Teach me to walk with You, trust You, and know You more deeply each day.

In Jesus' name, Amen.

A SIMPLE STEP TOWARD JESUS

If you have come this far, perhaps something in these stories has stirred your heart. Maybe it was a familiar struggle. Maybe it was a quiet question. Maybe it was a sense that there is more; more than what you have seen, more than what you have experienced so far. I want you to know this: Jesus is not far from you. He is not waiting for you to become better before you come to Him. He is not asking you to have everything figured out. He simply invites you to come.

The Bible says in Romans 10:9 (NKJV): *"That if you confess with your mouth the Lord Jesus and believe in your heart that God has raised Him from the dead, you will be saved."*

Receiving Him is not about saying a perfect prayer. It is about responding with a sincere heart. If you desire to begin this journey, you can pray a simple prayer like this:

A Prayer

Jesus,

I come to You just as I am.

I believe that You are the Son of God, that You died on the cross for my sins, and that You rose again to give me new life.

I confess that I have sinned and ask You to forgive me. Thank You for taking my place and paying the price I could never pay.

Today, I receive Your gift of salvation. Come into my life and be my Lord and my Savior.

Teach me to know You, to love You, to walk with You, and to trust You each day. Help me to follow You all the days of my life.

Thank You for loving me, forgiving me, and making me Your child.

In Jesus' name,

Amen.

If you have prayed this prayer; even quietly, even imperfectly, something has begun. Faith often starts with a simple step, as small as a mustard seed, but it grows into a lifelong journey with God. You do not have to walk this journey alone.

You can consider:

- Connecting with a local church.
- Speaking to someone who knows Jesus and can walk alongside you.
- Spending time reading the Bible and talking to God in prayer.

In the days ahead, you may discover that what began as a simple prayer becomes a living relationship with the One who knows you, loves you, and calls you His own.

There is more. And He is faithful to lead you into it.

May God bless you abundantly.

LET'S CONNECT

Thank you for reading *What You Say, Daddy?*

If this book has encouraged you, I would love to hear from you. Feel free to connect, share your reflections, or tell me how God has been speaking to you through your own journey.

WHATYOUSAYDADDY.VOICE

Instagram: *@whatyousaydaddy.voice*
Facebook: *What You Say, Daddy?*

Life may not always unfold the way we expect, but love, presence, and the words we speak into the lives of those entrusted to us will leave a legacy that lasts far beyond ourselves. After all, sometimes the most meaningful conversations begin with a gentle question: *"What You Say, Daddy?"*

ABOUT THE AUTHOR

Lex Khoo is a husband, father of three boys, and a follower of Jesus Christ.

For more than two decades, he has served in various ministries within the local church, including intercession, healing and deliverance, leadership development, and cell ministry. His passion is to see lives transformed through encounters with God's love, power, and presence.

Professionally, Lex has held senior leadership positions in the financial services industry, leading strategic initiatives and supporting business growth across global markets. He is an alumnus of Harvard Business School, Singapore Management University, Nanyang Technological University, and Tung Ling Bible School.

He is also the co-founder of Papa Foundation, a charitable initiative dedicated to supporting underprivileged children and communities.

Through this book, he hopes readers will discover that God still speaks, still leads, still heals, and still reveals His glory—even in the darkest moments of life.

More than any title or achievement, Lex considers himself just another ordinary man with an extraordinary God.

A READER'S GUIDE

This story takes place primarily in Singapore, with parts of the journey extending beyond its shores. The following brief notes provide a little background on some of the places, institutions, and organizations mentioned throughout the book.

Places

Singapore – *A city-state in Southeast Asia where most of this story takes place.*

Bugis – *A bustling shopping and commercial district in central Singapore.*

Geylang – *A district in Singapore known for its diverse local food culture and, in parts, its legally regulated red-light area.*

East Coast Park – *Singapore's largest seaside park, popular with families for beaches and outdoor activities.*

Hawker Centre – *A popular open-air food centre in Singapore offering a wide variety of affordable local dishes.*

Legoland Malaysia – *A family theme park in Johor, Malaysia, just across the border from Singapore.*

Mekong River – One of Asia's longest rivers, flowing through Cambodia and several countries.

Nagaland – *A state in north-eastern India, where Papa Foundation serves children and communities through education and outreach.*

Parkway Parade – *A well-known shopping mall on Singapore's East Coast that serves as a familiar landmark in the story.*

Serangoon – *A residential town in north-eastern Singapore where our family lived for many years.*

Institutions and Organizations

Harvard Business School – *The graduate business school of Harvard University in the United States.*

Nanyang Technological University (NTU) – *One of Singapore's leading universities, internationally recognized for engineering, science, business, and technology.*

Papa Foundation – *A charitable initiative co-founded by the author to support underprivileged children and communities through education and practical care.*

Singapore Management University (SMU) – *A public university in Singapore known for business, law, and social sciences.*

Tung Ling Bible School – *A Bible college in Singapore dedicated to equipping Christians for ministry and leadership.*

Made in the USA
Las Vegas, NV
05 August 2026

51840662R00125